# Entertainment WEEKLY
## COMMEMORATIVE EDITION

**1922-2018**

# Stan Lee
# A LIFE OF MARVEL

Stan Lee onstage at Spike TV's Scream Awards in Los Angeles in 2009 to accept the Comic-Con International's Icon Award. Just 13 titans of pop culture have received the award, including *Star Wars'* George Lucas and Lee's comic colleague Jack Kirby.

# Contents

**KEVIN FEIGE IN HIS OWN WORDS**

# HEROES MADE HUMAN

After helping create countless characters with seminal story lines, Stan Lee leaves behind a legacy bigger than them all. The president of Marvel Studios shares what "the Man" meant to him and to the world.

**BY KEVIN FEIGE** *As told to Anthony Breznican*

**YOU'VE HEARD THE LEGEND, WHICH I THINK** is true, that when Stan Lee was a young writer at Marvel Comics he was tired of doing the same old thing, and his wife, Joan, encouraged him to write the kind of stories he wanted to read.

That's what led to the Fantastic Four. Then Hulk, and Spider-Man. Then Iron Man, and the X-Men, and everything else. He realized in the midst of his amazing 1960s run what he was creating, that people were responding to his characters the same way he responded to ancient myths that he read as a kid, and he went, "Wait a minute. Lemme turn one of those characters into a hero." And we got Thor, we got Odin, we got Loki, we got Hela.

Stan was a charismatic, well-spoken cheerleader for his characters and for the medium of comics in general. Also, he was a very progressive storyteller. He took risks, and he wrote what he believed. You see the quote going around from one of his old "Stan's Soapbox" columns about how "a story without a message is like a man without a soul." Wow, is that true, and wow, that is apparent in all the stories he told.

What director Ryan Coogler was able to do with *Black Panther* would not exist if not for Stan Lee and artist Jack Kirby taking a quote-unquote "risk" bringing in an African—not even African-American, an *African*—character to their stories who was smarter and wealthier and more technologically advanced than any other hero. This was at the height of the civil rights movement, and that's astounding to me. He really had a good heart. He believed in the best of humanity. He also believed in the flaws of humanity, and that the flaws could be overcome.

Stan explored intimate questions and struggles, and he had a desire for understanding identity. It might be an obvious thing to say, but Stan Lee got his messages across in a way that was also compelling and entertaining and held an audience's interest.

Some of his lessons are unspoken. He didn't come to set and read the scripts and review the cuts. He came in, did a cameo that excited everybody and would let his work speak for itself. He was very nice in my interactions with him, including what ended up being my final conversation with him less than two weeks ago.

I went to his house to see him, and he reminisced about the cameos. We were talking about what was coming up, always looking to the future. Did he know that his time was running out? I don't know. In hindsight, he was slightly more wistful than I'd seen him before. He talked about the past more than I had ever heard him talk about the past. So maybe on some level, he knew.

When I sat down by his chair in our last meeting, the very first thing he said was: "I know you want me to *star* in the next movie, but I have to just stick to the cameos. You'll have to leave the starring roles to the other actors. I'm sorry."

He would show up to the movie sets game for anything. But one thing he would always do is try to add more lines. He always would joke—but not *really* joke—about wanting more lines, although he understood why we couldn't.

God forbid he would start to overshadow the hero. That was something a character like Stan Lee could easily do.

Kevin Feige and Stan Lee posed together at the premiere of 2018's *Avengers: Infinity War.*

# STAN LEE'S MOST ICONIC SUPERHEROES

Working with Jack Kirby, Steve Ditko and other artists in the 1960s, Lee breathed life into Iron Man, Spider-Man, the Fantastic Four and so many other superheroes who have dominated pop culture ever since. Long after Lee stopped writing Marvel comics himself, issues featuring his creations still carried the tagline "Stan Lee Presents," and his many appearances in Marvel movies cemented his creative legacy. His creations have passed through many hands since the '60s, but Lee brought unique elements to these world-famous characters. **BY CHRISTIAN HOLUB AND ALYSSA SMITH**

## SPIDER-MAN

One of the few Marvel superheroes Lee did not co-create with Jack Kirby would end up being the company's most popular character of all. After Kirby tried and failed to come up with an engaging design for a spider-themed superhero, Lee turned instead to Steve Ditko, the other artistic titan of Marvel's classic era. While Ditko provided the stunning costume design and acrobatic fight scenes, Lee provided the character's personality. Whenever Peter Parker puts on that red mask, he shifts from an outcast nerd to a wisecracking daredevil, a perfect distillation of Lee's own legendary humor. As journalist Sean Howe wrote in *Marvel Comics: The Untold Story*, "Lee's brilliant touch was to have Parker deliver a nonstop parade of corny jokes when he was in the Spider-Man costume: a convincing manifestation of obsessive nervous thinking, yes, but more importantly an effective mood-lightener."

Over the years Spider-Man's origin has been told and retold many, many times. But no adaptation has matched the efficient storytelling of *Amazing Fantasy* #15, nor has anyone ever come up with a better summation of Spider-Man's heroism than Lee's nine legendary words from that issue: "With great power then also must come—great responsibility!"

The popularity of Spider-Man cannot be overstated; three live-action versions of the webslinger have appeared in seven solo movies since 2002 grossing more than $4.8 billion worldwide, starting with Tobey Maguire (pictured).

## FANTASTIC FOUR

The legend goes that Marvel publisher Martin Goodman was playing golf in 1961 with a rival executive from DC who bragged to him about their bestselling comic, *Justice League of America*. Goodman returned to the Marvel offices (or Timely, as the company was called until 1962) and ordered Lee, at that point one of his only employees in the comic department, to come up with a superhero team of their own. Lee teamed up with artist Jack Kirby, who decades earlier had co-created Captain America for Goodman, and together

they devised a superhero comic that would change everything.

It was on Fantastic Four that Lee and Kirby developed what came to be known as the Marvel Method—a creative process in which Lee would come up with a short plot outline, then Kirby would design and illustrate a comic based on a mixture of that synopsis and his own ideas, and then Lee would return to fill in the dialogue and captions. Though this method would prove quite successful at allowing Lee to write so many comics at once, it also created an ambivalence about which ideas

belonged to which creator. This led to tension over the years, and after their partnership dissolved, Kirby and Lee would later offer up conflicting versions of the creation and development of Fantastic Four. But in its prime their creative collaboration worked spectacularly. Over the first 100 issues of Fantastic Four, Lee and Kirby introduced readers to many now-iconic characters and concepts, from Black Panther to the Inhumans to the world-eating Galactus. While Kirby illustrated terrifying villains, out-of-this-world monsters and kinetic superhero brawls, Lee provided the

essential voices of the characters. Unlike the Justice League, the Fantastic Four was a family, and they acted like it—complete with all the angst, infighting and self-doubt that would come to define Marvel characters and set them apart from their genre peers.

The superfamily has had several big-screen versions, starting with an unreleased B-movie produced originally in 1994. Pictured here from the 2005 film *Fantastic Four,* Jessica Alba, Ioan Gruffudd, Chris Evans (the actor would later join the Marvel Cinematic Universe in the role of Captain America) and Michael Chiklis.

## SILVER SURFER

There's no ambivalence about who first created the high-flying Sentinel of the Spaceways. When Kirby came back with illustrations for the three-part "Galactus Trilogy" story he and Lee were working on in Fantastic Four, Lee was astonished to see a character that hadn't been in his original outline: a silver figure riding a surfboard. Eventually, though, Silver Surfer would become the focus of some of Lee's most personal and introspective work. While Kirby had intended the character to be a cold Spock-like alien being, Lee really related to the character's nobility and his rage at being trapped on Earth in the wake of the "Galactus Trilogy" (perhaps analogous to Lee's own occasional dissatisfaction at being stuck writing comics when he originally wanted to be a novelist). Lee took the character for his own, writing an 18-issue comic and advising other writers not to use him.

In 2007 moviegoers had the chance to see the Silver Surfer on the screen, embodied by creature actor Doug Jones.

## THOR

Provenance on who can claim credit for this founding member of the Avengers is shaky. After all, the legends of the Norse gods have been retold for centuries. Yet before the superhero ever hefted Mjolnir in August 1962's issue of *Journey into Mystery* #83, at least two prior versions of the thunder god had appeared in comic-book form. Five years earlier Kirby illustrated a version of Thor during his stint at DC Comics in a story titled "The Magic Hammer," featuring a barrel-chested hero trying to recover his stolen hammer from his brother Loki (sound familiar?). And Ditko had also penned a hero whose hammer granted him divine powers for Charlton Comics in 1959.

Yet the Marvel hero, portrayed on the big screen by Chris Hemsworth in three solo outings and the Avengers films to date, has resonated most with audiences. Lee's younger brother Larry Lieber first scripted the character under guidance from Lee, who said, "I dreamed up Thor years ago because I wanted to create the biggest, most powerful superhero of all, and I figured who can be bigger than a god?" Thor was one of the first heroes Lee tried to bring to the silver screen in the 1990s. He pitched Sam Raimi—the two would eventually collaborate on 2002's *Spider-Man*—but it was not meant to be. Movie executives at the time weren't convinced that superhero films made money.

## THE HULK

While Kirby has said his inspiration for the Hulk was seeing a woman lift a car to save her child (showing how people can perform amazing feats of strength when angry or desperate enough), Lee said he was directly influenced by classic monster stories like *Dr. Jekyll and Mr. Hyde* and particularly *Frankenstein,* and imbued the pathos into the character's DNA.

"I've always had a soft spot in my heart for the Frankenstein monster. No one could ever convince me that he was the bad guy," Lee wrote in a 1974 book called *Origins of Marvel Comics.* That balance between the Hulk's unmatchable strength and his pity-inducing tortured lifestyle has helped the character endure in pop culture. Even today, in MCU films like *The Avengers* and *Thor: Ragnarok,* the Hulk's astonishing power is always juxtaposed with Bruce Banner's fear of losing control and the fear that his attempts at heroism will end up unleashing a monster on an unsuspecting populace.

Today Mark Ruffalo (right) stars as the Hulk's alter ego, Dr. Banner.

**ANT-MAN**
One of several characters imbued with creature powers that Lee would co-create with Kirby, when the microscopic hero Hank Pym first appeared in the January 1962 issue *Tales to Astonish!*, sans super-suit, he was not a hit. Even after Ant-Man helped found the Avengers along with Iron Man, Thor, the Hulk and his new love inter-est and pinch hitter Janet Van Dyne, who

fought baddies under the moniker the Wasp, sales sagged. So Lee recycled the idea, in the other direction. "I liked Ant-Man, but he never really became one of our bestselling heroes," explained Lee in 2015. "After a while we decided to change the character—make him really big to fit in the Avengers with Thor and Hulk and Iron Man—and he became Giant-Man."
    Constant reinvention and expansion

became a hallmark of the teeny tiny character, who appeared in occasional cameos between 1963 and 1979. *Marvel Premiere* #47 in April 1979 introduced a brand-new incarnation: Scott Lang, a criminal with a heart of gold who steals one of Pym's Ant-Man costumes and eventually becomes the next hero—a plotline popularized in Paul Rudd's 2015 outing *Ant-Man*.

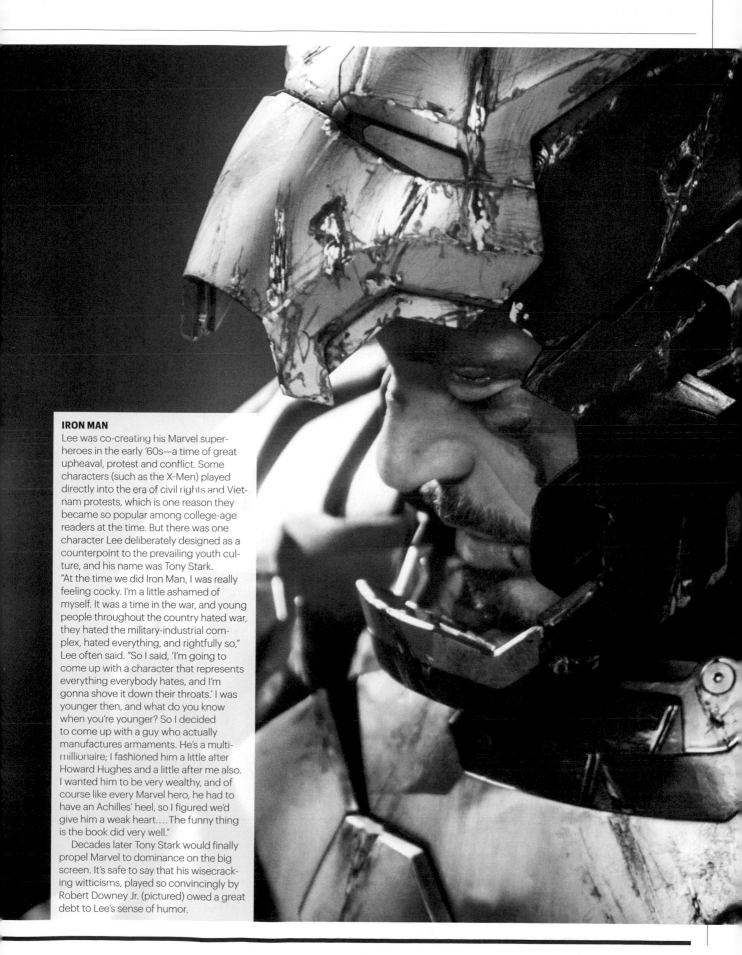

## IRON MAN

Lee was co-creating his Marvel super-heroes in the early '60s—a time of great upheaval, protest and conflict. Some characters (such as the X-Men) played directly into the era of civil rights and Vietnam protests, which is one reason they became so popular among college-age readers at the time. But there was one character Lee deliberately designed as a counterpoint to the prevailing youth culture, and his name was Tony Stark.

"At the time we did Iron Man, I was really feeling cocky. I'm a little ashamed of myself. It was a time in the war, and young people throughout the country hated war, they hated the military-industrial complex, hated everything, and rightfully so," Lee often said. "So I said, 'I'm going to come up with a character that represents everything everybody hates, and I'm gonna shove it down their throats.' I was younger then, and what do you know when you're younger? So I decided to come up with a guy who actually manufactures armaments. He's a multi-millionaire; I fashioned him a little after Howard Hughes and a little after me also. I wanted him to be very wealthy, and of course like every Marvel hero, he had to have an Achilles' heel, so I figured we'd give him a weak heart.…The funny thing is the book did very well."

Decades later Tony Stark would finally propel Marvel to dominance on the big screen. It's safe to say that his wisecracking witticisms, played so convincingly by Robert Downey Jr. (pictured) owed a great debt to Lee's sense of humor.

# Superheroes Welcome

**DAREDEVIL**

The Marvel Method came into full force during the creation of the Devil of Hell's Kitchen, with Lee co-creating the blind hero this time with artist Bill Everett. Kirby assisted with the design of the character Matt Murdock, in particular coming up with the idea of Daredevil's weapon, the billy club, as well as illustrating the cover of April 1964's *Daredevil* #1.

Yet what Lee brought to this particular comic book, in addition to sketching out the working-class background of its hero, was the setting: a gritty, dark backdrop and a clear vision of a lived-in city rife with villains to stop and civilians to save. That vision remained intact when in the 1980s the character's background evolved dramatically under the writing of Frank Miller. With Spider-Man's villain William Fisk, aka the Kingpin, as Murdock's new nemesis, the seedy underbelly of the most urban, densely populated section of New York still speaks to audiences. Above, Charlie Cox as Daredevil from the Netflix show that ran for three seasons between 2015 and 2018.

## DOCTOR STRANGE

One of Lee's signature solutions to keeping all the different comics he was writing straight in his head was using a lot of alliteration, which is why many Marvel superheroes begin their first and last names with the same letter. When it came to Doctor Strange, however, Lee really turned the alliteration up a notch. The character's name was not just Stephen Strange; his many titles included the "Sorcerer Supreme" and "Master of the Mystic Arts," and he resided in a "Sanctum Sanctorum." Beyond that, when it came time for the character to pull out a spell or magic incantation, Lee gave him exclamations like "by the Hoary Hosts of Hoggoth!" or weapons like the "Wand of Waatomb" and the "Eye of Agamotto." Combined with Steve Ditko's psychedelic art, this wording gave the character a mystical aura that entranced college-aged readers at the time. Many of those terms made it into the recent *Doctor Strange* movie starring Benedict Cumberbatch, proving that the magical power of Lee's alliteration can stand the test of time.

Sophie Turner as Jean Grey, Kodi Smit-McPhee as Nightcrawler and Tye Sheridan as Cyclops.

James Marsden as Cyclops and Famke Janssen as Jean Grey.

## X-MEN

The X-Men were latecomers to the Marvel universe, arriving in the wake of the Fantastic Four, Spider-Man, Hulk, Thor and so many others. By that point Lee was tired of coming up with some new variant of radiation to explain each new character's superpowers. With the X-Men, he finally came up with a simple solution to the problem: Just call them "mutants." These characters would be born with their powers, no radioactive bombs or spiders needed. As a result of having natural powers, these characters looked a lot like normal humans, except for one trait that set them apart.

This became a fertile metaphor in the era of civil rights protests. Despite saving the world on a regular basis, the X-Men faced only prejudice and xenophobia from their fellow man. They were fighting mutant-hating maniacs at the same time that white supremacists were bombing the Sixteenth Street Baptist Church in Birmingham, Ala. From a certain angle, the nonviolent Professor X and the more separatist Magneto could even be construed as metaphors for Martin Luther King Jr. and Malcolm X.

The X-Men were not the most popular of Lee's collaborations with Kirby, but over time they would grow to become Marvel superstars. Later creators would diversify the characters and complicate the civil rights metaphor, but from the very beginning, Lee imbued the X-Men with a strong sense of social justice that they retain to this day. His creations went on to spawn one of the first major movie franchises in 2000, with a dozen sequels, prequels, origin stories and flashbacks.

Patrick Stewart as Professor X.

Ben Hardy as Angel.

## BLACK PANTHER

Lee never wrote a solo Black Panther series, but it was he and Kirby who introduced T'Challa in *Fantastic Four* #52-53. In contrast to the prior history of mainstream comics, which had almost exclusively portrayed Africans solely as brutal savages, the Black Panther was an eloquent leader, a brilliant scientist and a strategic fighter who managed to outwit the Fantastic Four, Marvel's pride and joy. Wakanda was also unique; while the Thing expected to see what had been "in a million jungle movies," he and his team were surprised to find a highly advanced African country that hid its technological superiority behind an illusion and had successfully resisted colonization.

All these elements, part of the character from the start, have carried over into the modern MCU films, where Chadwick Boseman's Black Panther (pictured) held his own against the Avengers in *Captain America: Civil War* and also fought off Thanos's alien armies in *Infinity War*. Ryan Coogler's Black Panther film, hailed as a new high watermark for diverse storytelling, is also a continuation of Lee's legacy. Back at a time when there were no other black superheroes to speak of, Lee had T'Challa deliver a brief but powerful manifesto of representation to his enemy Klaw: "I exist!"

Stan Lee served during World War II with the designation "playwright," undertaking various communications tasks.

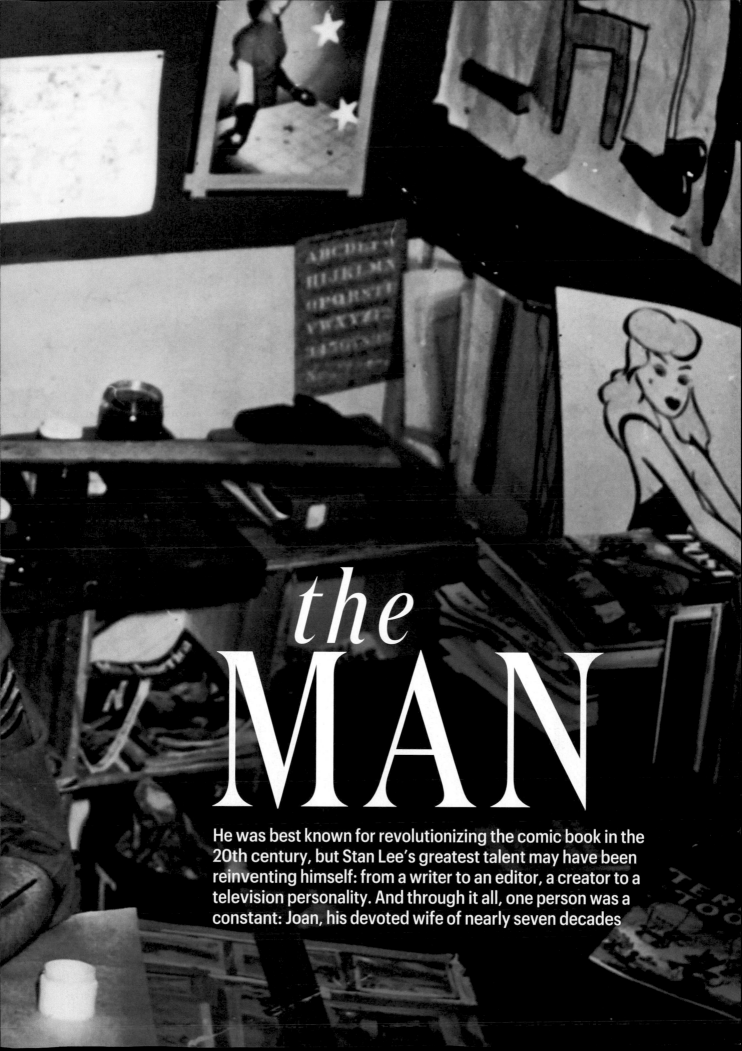

# *the* MAN

He was best known for revolutionizing the comic book in the 20th century, but Stan Lee's greatest talent may have been reinventing himself: from a writer to an editor, a creator to a television personality. And through it all, one person was a constant: Joan, his devoted wife of nearly seven decades

# Origin Story

FROM HIS
DEPRESSION-ERA
BEGINNINGS IN NEW
YORK CITY TO HIS
PIONEERING WORK
AT MARVEL COMICS
AND BEYOND—A
LOOK BACK AT A
LIFE WELL-LIVED.
*By Rich Sands*

◄

Stan Lee in London in
February 1979. Two years
later he began developing
movie and television
properties for Marvel.

**STAN LEE WAS ALWAYS A BIT OF A SHOW-OFF.**
Growing up in New York City during the
Depression, he would indulge his doting
mother's requests to read to her. "Being
the ham that I am, I enjoyed doing that,
imagining I was on some Broadway stage
reading for a vast, entranced audience," he
wrote in his 2002 autobiography *Excelsior!:
The Amazing Life of Stan Lee*. This flair for
performance would serve him well
through his 95 years, as he used a combination of skillful storytelling and
self-promotion to become the most cele-
brated comic-book writer in the world, as
popular in some circles as the ubiquitous
heroes he conjured up.

In addition to feeding his creativity,
reading also provided an escape from a
gloomy home life. He was born Stanley

Martin Lieber on Dec. 28, 1922, to Jewish Romanian immigrants Jack and Celia, and he recalled that his parents frequently squabbled over Jack's inability to find steady work. "I always felt sorry for my father," Lee wrote. "He was a good man, honest and caring. He wanted the best for his family, as most parents do. But the times were against him.... Seeing the demoralizing effect that his unemployment had on his spirit, making him feel that he just wasn't needed, gave me a feeling I've never been able to shake."

When Stanley's brother Larry was born in 1931, the tension only intensified. Stanley was encouraged to finish high school early so that he could get a full-time job. While still a student he worked as an obituary writer for a wire service and as a hospital PR scribe, but neither job satisfied his storytelling itch. A fateful family connection led him on a path that would end up revolutionizing the world of pop culture.

Immediately upon graduating from DeWitt Clinton High School in the Bronx in 1939, Lee got a job with Timely Comics, part of a magazine publishing company owned by Martin Goodman, the husband of Stanley's cousin Jean. He was hired for $8 a week, helping Captain America creators Joe Simon and Jack Kirby with various office and production tasks.

As the popularity of comic books grew, Stanley was soon asked to write some short stories in the books. Before long he was pitching in with increasing frequency. "I wrote whatever they told me to write the way they told me to write it," he told *Entertainment Weekly* in 2003. "It didn't matter: war stories, crime, westerns, horror, humor; I wrote everything."

He used several pseudonyms but most frequently went with Stan Lee. "I didn't want to use the name Stanley Martin Lieber because I was saving that for the great American novel—which I never wrote," he said in the 2010 documentary *With Great Power: The Stan Lee Story.* (Eventually he would have his name legally changed.)

When Simon and Kirby left Timely, Lee,

Lee with wife Joan in 1977 (left) and with his daughter Joan Celia Lee in 2016. Opposite: Lee (in striped shirt) with artist John Romita, who in 2002 entered the Will Eisner Comic Book Hall of Fame.

still just 18, was given the editor's reins. But his first tenure in charge was short-lived. In 1942, as the United States was getting into World War II, Lee enlisted. While in the Army he rotated through several domestic bases, serving in a variety of writing and PR roles with the Signal Corps, with the hifalutin classification of playwright. (Only a handful of soldiers got this role; among the others were Oscar-winning director Frank Capra and Theodor Geisel, aka famed children's book author Dr. Seuss.) Lee's gigs included writing a marching song for the Army Finance Department (sample lyric: "Clerks alert, guarding our books from blunder, Payroll forms clutter the floor") and conceiving a poster cautioning soldiers about the dangers of venereal disease.

When the war ended, Lee returned to New York and resumed his role producing a stream of comic-book stories for Timely. In 1947 he fell in love with a charming English hat model and actress, Joan Boocock. She was already wed, rather ambivalently, to another man, so a persistent Lee helped her get a divorce in Reno. He then married her on the spot.

The couple had a daughter, Joan Celia (aka J.C.), in 1950, who as an adult would love to remind people that she, and not any comic-book character, was her father's greatest creation. (Stan and Joan had a second daughter, Jan, in 1953, but she tragically died just a few days after her birth.)

On the work front, Lee would soon learn the fickle nature of the comics business. In the mid-1950s the hysterical anti-comics crusade of psychiatrist Fredric Wertham—who claimed that violence, sex and horror in the books led to juvenile delinquency—prompted the birth of the Comics Code Authority, which meticulously policed the pages for objectionable material. Sales sank (competition for readers' attention from television was also to blame), and Goodman had Lee lay off the Timely staff. "That was like one of the worst moments of my life," he said in *With Great Power.* "Because these weren't just artists and writers who worked for me, these were people who were like my closest friends."

BY THE START OF THE NEXT DECADE, THE business began to rebound, thanks in large

part to DC Comics' popular Justice League of America, a union of Superman, Batman, Wonder Woman and others. When Goodman reportedly heard of the success from his friend Jack Liebowitz, DC's president, he tasked Lee with creating a similar group of superfriends for Timely.

At the time, Lee was contemplating leaving the company. Now 38, he had started to wonder if he'd ended up in a career that was still considered juvenile entertainment. He told his wife of his plans to quit and received profound advice. "She was completely supportive, but then she added something I hadn't thought of," he wrote. "'You know, Stan, if Martin wants you to create a new group of superheroes, this could be a chance for you to do it the way you've always wanted to. You could dream up plots that have more depth and substance to them, and create characters who have interesting personalities, who speak like real people.'"

Inspired and rejuvenated, Lee set out to create his own superhero squad. The result, a far cry from the colorful yet emotionless members of the Justice League, was the Fantastic Four, a group of astronauts who received bizarre abilities after exposure to cosmic rays. But instead of embracing their powers, they found their lives thrown into chaos. Sure, they would fight villains and save the world, but they weren't necessarily happy about it. "For once I wanted to write stories that wouldn't insult the intelligence of an older reader," Lee recalled, "stories with interesting characterization, more realistic dialogue and plots that hadn't been recycled a thousand times before."

His creative fire now rekindled, Lee worked with superstar artists such as Jack Kirby and Steve Ditko, who would plot and draw the stories based on Lee's concepts. Lee and his colleagues went on a historic tear over the next several years as Timely was rechristened Marvel Comics, creating a string of iconic heroes: the Hulk, Spider-Man, Thor, the X-Men, Iron Man, the Avengers, Black Panther, Daredevil and others. Lee also had his brother Larry Lieber as a key member of the team,

▲
A 1961 edition of *The Fantastic Four,* by Stan Lee and Jack Kirby, which introduced the group as a team. Right: Spider-Man's first appearance, in *Amazing Fantasy* #15, August 1962. Opposite: Lee ca. 1980.

working on Thor and Iron Man, among others. Lee admitted he may have gone too far in trying to avoid nepotism. "I sometimes feel, in an effort to be extremely fair, I've bent over backward not to favor him over any other artists or writers because he's my brother," he wrote later. "Thinking back about it, I feel I've done him a disservice." (Now 87, Larry only retired from drawing *The Amazing Spider-Man* newspaper strip in September 2018.)

Among Lee's innovations were to have his heroes live in the real world, mainly New York City, rather than in fictional locales like DC's Metropolis. He also popularized the idea of a shared universe linking Marvel's many titles with story lines connecting and characters guest-starring in one another's books.

By the mid-1960s Marvel was selling upwards of 40 million copies a year. Comics became incredibly popular on college campuses and slowly began to lose the stigma from Fredric Wertham's histrionic campaign. "I guess there's a certain irony to the fact that some of the children who had comic books taken away from them when they were 5 years old, when they were in college, when they were 20 years old or so, they were inviting me to come and speak at their college," Lee noted in *With Great Power.*

This was the beginning of Stan Lee's emergence as a celebrity, a persona he zealously worked to promote. In 1966 a glowing *New York Herald Tribune* profile called him "an ultra-Madison Avenue, rangy lookalike of Rex Harrison. He's got that horsy jaw and humorous eyes, thinning but tasteful gray hair, the brightest-colored Ivy League wardrobe in captivity and a deep suntan that comes from working every Tuesday, Thursday, Saturday and Sunday on his suburban terrace, cranking out three complete Marvel mags weekly."

Significant attention has since been paid to how the Marvel artists, particularly industry legends like Kirby and Ditko, weren't given their fair share of the credit at the time, while Lee happily usurped them as the face of the company. In later years Lee acknowledged his colleagues, though sometimes with a patronizing tone. As he said in his autobiography: "I'm willing to call myself co-creator of all the characters

I've dreamed up, thereby sharing a grateful world's plaudits and accolades with the artists who did me so proud."

**AFTER DECADES OF LIVING ON LONG ISLAND** and in New York City, Lee eventually moved to Los Angeles to help bring Marvel characters to screen. "I've always thought of myself as being in show business," he told *Time* in 1979. "It's just taken the world a long time to realize it." On the animated TV series *Spider-Man and His Amazing Friends*, which aired in the early 1980s, Lee served as narrator, foreshadowing his later trademark of making cameo appearances in all of Marvel's films.

Many of the early live-action creations were forgettable—ironically they lacked the signature heart and humanity of their comic-book source material—but *The Incredible Hulk*, starring Bill Bixby and Lou Ferrigno as the Jekyll and Hyde sides of the character, was a breakout hit on CBS from 1977 to '82. It wasn't until the start of the 21st century, however, with films such as *X-Men* and *Spider-Man*, that the true Hollywood potential of Marvel's characters was fully unleashed.

That turnaround followed Marvel's troubled corporate struggles and ultimate bankruptcy in 1996. In the wake of that turmoil Lee left the company and formed digital superhero ventures Stan Lee Media and later POW! Entertainment, neither of which duplicated his previous success. (Stan Lee Media was felled by financial improprieties, though Lee was not connected.)

By then Lee had secured a significant lifetime contract with Marvel that included an annual salary, 10 percent of the company's film and TV profits, and the title chairman emeritus. In addition, he was allowed to continue to pursue his non-Marvel ventures. He later sued Marvel, alleging it hadn't honored his profit-sharing deal, and when it was finally settled in 2005, Lee kept his salary but instead of profits was given an undisclosed amount. "It was very emotional," Lee told *60 Minutes* in 2002, pointing out that he'd always been a work-for-hire employee and

▲
Superhero sandwich! Lee with actors Eric Kramer (Thor) and Lou Ferrigno (the Hulk) on the set of the NBC movie *The Incredible Hulk Returns* in 1988.

had never had ownership over his numerous creations. "I guess what happened was I was really hurt. We had always had this great relationship, the company and me. I felt I was a part of it."

Even if Marvel resented the deal, they knew that it was an unwinnable PR battle. Lee had become the most famous comic-book personality on the planet, constantly swarmed by adoring throngs of fans at conventions, and a pop-culture mainstay, with guest appearances on shows such as *The Simpsons* and *The Big Bang Theory* along with his dozens of cameos in Marvel films, TV series and cartoons.

In his final years Lee became more of a figurehead for both POW! and Marvel, though he kept a high profile at premieres and conventions. He and Joan lived in Los Angeles for nearly four decades, doting on each other, as she seemed to revel in his playful ribbing about her interest in shopping—and ambivalence toward comics. "Perhaps that's one of the things that makes for a good relationship," Stan wrote. "I can be relaxed, and Joanie isn't bored listening to me talk about things in which she has no interest."

Though she largely gave up her acting career when they were married, Joan did voice work for some Marvel cartoons in the 1990s and wrote a romance novel, *The Pleasure Palace,* in 1987. Their daughter J.C., now 68, did some acting after the family moved to L.A. She was frequently at her father's side at public events and remained fiercely protective of him as he aged.

Joan Lee died in July 2017—the couple had been married for nearly 70 years—and it's surely not coincidental that Stan's own health and well-being almost immediately went into steep decline. In his last year, disputed allegations of fraud by two of Lee's business associates and even charges of elder abuse on the part of his former manager arose, putting a sordid spotlight on the coda of his life.

Yet in his final public appearance, at the April 2018 premiere of *Avengers: Infinity War*, Lee still demonstrated his knack for well-timed and good-natured immodesty. "I want to thank [my fans] for having spent all these years coming to see my cameos," Lee told a reporter on the red carpet, "and of course watching the movie with it."

◀ Hulking out in Vegas with Iron Man's Hulkbuster in 2017.

▲ Lee puckering up to his friendly neighborhood Spider-Man in 2011.

▼ Holding court at the *Thor* premiere in 2011.

# the
# COMICS

During his many years in the business, Stan Lee co-created dozens of original (and some not-so-original) comic-book characters, at first in genres spanning from westerns to detective stories. His greatest hits, of course, were the out-of-this-world superheroes with whom readers connected so deeply. The secret? All of them were flawed—as human as Lee himself

# THE STORY AS HE SAW IT

In 2017 Stan Lee wrote an introduction to a *Life* special issue about superheroes, sharing some of his thoughts on why the comicbook genre has endured through the ages

**THE TERM "SUPERHERO" CAME INTO USAGE** barely 80 years ago. It all started when National Comics (later to become DC Comics) published *Superman,* the creation of Jerry Siegel and Joe Shuster. Suddenly, in the realm of adventure fiction, we had a hero who was superstrong, could leap over a skyscraper and run faster than a speeding train.

After Superman, it was as though the dam had been broken. Suddenly Timely Comics (later to become Marvel) introduced the Human Torch, a hero created by Carl Burgos, who could burst into flame and fly. They also brought forth the Sub-Mariner, Prince of Atlantis, by Bill Everett. He could breathe under water, was superstrong and had the power of flight.

As events led up to World War II, the publishers all got on the patriotic bandwagon. Suddenly the superheroes fought more than gang leaders and crazed assassins. Now they had the Nazis to conquer. Among the many patriotic heroes, Timely's Captain America, a shield-slinging supersoldier created by Joe Simon and Jack Kirby, was one of the most successful.

But the superheroes were more than a wartime fad. Even in later years, in peacetime, they became the most popular of all comicbook characters. In seeking a reason for their amazing and long-term popularity, I've come up with a theory . . .

Almost without exception, every young child has been weaned on fairy tales, stories involving witches and monsters and demons and magicians and giants—perfect fodder to feed a youngster's sense of wonder and magic.

Naturally, in a short time we become too old for fairy tales. However, I believe we never lose our love for those tales of people who are bigger than life. They are faced with all sorts of monsters and dangers that are likewise bigger *and* far more colorful than anything in real life. And of course, we also have the birth of the supervillains.

Regarding the tremendous popularity of today's comicbooks, it's interesting to realize that during the early days of comics parents tried their best to steer their children away from comicbooks. Many of them were convinced that because comics were illustrated stories, the youngsters would be so caught up in the pictures that they would never become good readers.

Being aware of that concern, I made it a point to actually use college-level vocabulary on all of Marvel's comics. If a youngster wasn't familiar with a word, he'd learn what it meant by its use in the sentence or, if he had to go to a dictionary to look it up, that wasn't the worst thing that could happen.

Later, as schools looked into the effects of comicbook reading, they found that comics were actually an aid in making youngsters into readers because kids had to be able to read and understand the text in order to get the full impact of the story itself.

Today, comics are more popular than ever. But there is one serious problem that I've been relentlessly trying to solve. Too many people write "comicbook" as two words. That means a funny book, which is not its intention. It should always be written as one word, "comicbook," which refers to a specific type of reading material. Don't ever let me catch you spelling it wrong!*

Can't write any more just now. Dr. Octopus is trying to break into my study and I've got to contact Spidey while there's still time! (And remember: Never omit the hyphen in Spider-Man's name or he might just ignore your call.) Excelsior!

*Editor's note: Sorry, Stan, our copy editors overruled us here!

A montage of comic books from the Silver Age.

> **"I believe we never lose our love for those tales of people who are bigger than life"**
>
> —STAN LEE

JOE QUESADA
IN HIS
OWN
WORDS

# STATE OF THE ART

A titan of Marvel recalls meeting Stan Lee as a young comic-book editor. Now he remembers his mentor as a friend—and a brilliant writer.

**BY JOE QUESADA** *As told to Kevin P. Sullivan*

I BECAME AWARE OF A MAN NAMED STAN LEE at the age of 8. My father introduced me to him—believe it or not. He had read something in the *Daily News* about this guy named Stan Lee. At the time, Stan was writing a comic that dealt with the evils of drug addiction, so my father—like most fathers would—thought to himself, "What a great way to teach my son about the evils of drug addiction: a comic book!"

While I never got addicted to drugs, it did end up costing my father a lot more in the long run. I got addicted to comic books.

What kept me coming back after that first issue was the unbridled imagination of Marvel Comics. It was his column "Stan's Soapbox," where he'd talk directly to the readers. It made us feel like we were a part of the process of making the sausage. The Soapboxes would have all of these incredible messages about his views on society, on what's right and wrong, what's good and bad. He wasn't talking down to the readers, but he was literally like a second father in a lot of ways.

It's hard to say when I first met Stan. As a working professional, I probably ran into him occasionally at conventions, but we never had a proper introduction then. My first real, real meeting with Stan was over the phone. In the late '90s I'm suddenly an editor at Marvel, running the

◄
Marvel Entertainment's
chief creative officer Joe
Quesada introduced
Disney Infinity 2.0 in 2014.

▲
In 2012 Quesada posed
with Stan Lee, head of
Marvel TV Jeph Loeb
and Spider-Man himself.

Marvel Knights imprint as well as working full-time as an artist there. I'm a bit nervous when I get the first pitches for those initial four books because I don't know if I'm doing this right. So I cold-call Stan. You're not supposed to cold-call Stan, but I do it anyway, and I ask if he would look at the outlines for the first stories. He gets back to me the next day with brilliant, minor touches on everything. It just shifted things and made them more Marvel. I'm realizing, "That's what makes a story Marvel. That's how we make it more relatable."

That formula of his is also why Marvel characters stand the test of time better than any other characters. Our Peter Parker has changed. He's not the pencil-necked kid with the pocket protector, but he's still the same guy. We've just moved him through time. That's the power of what Stan created, that subtle paradigm shift from focusing on the costume to focusing on the person.

What made Stan different was his real sense of the popular culture and the youth movement. He never looked at later generations and thought, "They don't know what they're doing. We used to do it better in our day." Stan was the person saying, "You guys are doing a million times better." When he started the Marvel Universe with his collaborators, he wasn't a 20-year-old dude. He was well into his life, yet he was so interested in politics and what was going on in society and the civil rights movement. In fact, Stan banned cigarette smoking in the Marvel offices in the '60s. That's how far ahead of it he was. You can't write stories like that unless you are.

If you look at the history of Marvel, it's been ups and downs. But when we're doing our best is when we're communicating with our readers and doing exactly what Stan did. I saw this clearly when I was editor in chief. Stan left us an instruction booklet on how to fix this company. It's metaphorically in his drawer. All you had to do was look at his books.

# A History of Comics

FROM THE SPLASH PAGE TO THE SILVER SCREEN, THE ART FORM HAS A STORIED LEGACY— ONE IN WHICH **STAN LEE** PLAYED MUCH MORE THAN A CAMEO ROLE

◄
Stan Lee with his larger-than-life webslinger in 1996.

**IT'S A BIRD! IT'S A PLANE! IT'S A . . . VAGRANT** turned villain hell-bent on total annihilation! Yes, it seems hard to believe now, but the origin story of comics as we know them starts not with a superhero but with a superbad dude.

"The Super-Man," as he was originally known, was the brainchild of Cleveland natives Jerry Siegel and Joe Shuster. He first appeared in 1933 in Siegel's self-published magazine *Science Fiction: The Advance Guard of Future Civilizations*, as a transient who is pulled from a breadline and used for scientific experimentation, bestowing him with superpowers. But instead of using his newfound psychic abilities to, say, rescue a cat from a tree, the Super-Man instead enslaves mankind before meeting a tragic end.

Siegel (the writer) and Shuster (the artist) spent years tinkering with their creation as they tried to sell the strip to different publishers, along the way drawing inspiration from characters like John Carter, the Scarlet Pimpernel and Zorro.

When Superman finally made his comic-book debut in 1938's *Action Comics* #1, he changed the landscape of comics forever. Superman, as a champion for the oppressed, in his first 13-page story, saved a wrongly convicted woman from death row, stopped a wife beater, rescued his colleague and love interest Lois Lane from lecherous hoodlums and tracked down a corrupt senator who was in the pocket of a munitions magnate. He challenged authority and fought for the working class throughout his early adventures, and the populist element of the character made him resonate with readers who were just starting to recover from the hardships of the Great Depression.

*Action Comics* #1 (published by the company that would later be known as DC Comics) is widely considered the starting point for the golden age of comics (roughly 1938-50), and the popularity of Superman signaled the birth of a new superhero genre that would dominate the medium for decades.

## HEROES NEEDED

The year after Superman's debut proved pivotal for the nascent category. Not only was the world introduced to the caped crusader known as Batman, but a pair of Marvels would make a big splash. Fawcett Comics' Captain Marvel joined the scene, becoming one of the most popular superheroes of the following decade (even outselling Superman), and Timely Publications' *Marvel Comics* #1 introduced a new superhero universe that would grow to become an entertainment juggernaut. *Marvel Comics* captivated readers with its tales of the Human Torch, a flaming android, and the Sub-Mariner, an antihero from the sea.

It was around that same time that Timely brought on a new employee in its Midtown Manhattan office: a recent high school graduate from the Bronx named Stanley Lieber. (His cousin-in-law Martin Goodman happened to own the company.) Stan Lee, as he would later become known, was assigned as a gofer to the comics division, where he'd run errands for Joe Simon and Jack Kirby, the creators of Captain America. As Timely began running more and more comics, Lee was eventually allowed to write his own strips because, as he mused to *Entertainment Weekly* in 2003, "I knew the difference between a declarative sentence and a baseball bat."

Lee made his comics writing debut with a bit of text-filler in the May 1941 issue of *Captain America Comics* #3. He was 18 years old. Later that year, when Simon and Kirby left Timely, Lee, callow though he may have been, was promoted to the role of editor. It was meant to be an interim gig, but aside from a tour of duty during World War II (in which he served as— what else—a writer), Lee remained at the post for more than three decades.

Meanwhile, with the war raging, comics were quickly becoming an important propaganda tool for the Office of War Information and the Writers' War Board (WWB). Comics publishers who agreed to work with the WWB received regular pitches from the WWB's Comics Committee, which would develop story arcs and characters with specific propaganda goals in mind. With strict wartime paper rationing in place, cooperating with the WWB was also a smart way for publishers to face fewer restrictions on paper usage.

The combination of inspiring, hopeful

◀

Lee in Marvel's
New York office
in 1980.

stories, unbreakable heroes and an inexpensive, highly portable format made comics very popular with U.S. soldiers. It's estimated that at least 44 percent of soldiers were regularly reading comic books during the war. (*Captain Marvel Adventures* sold more than 14 million copies alone in 1944.) Comics were making a mark as a quintessentially American art form that heavily and unapologetically pushed American values, introducing patriotic figures like Captain America, Captain Marvel and Wonder Woman, who endure today.

### MARVEL ASCENDING

By the early 1960s Timely had changed its name to Atlas, and inspired by the strong preliminary sales figures for DC's *Justice League of America*—a superteam consisting of Batman, Superman, Wonder Woman and others—Goodman asked Lee to create a similar squad for his imprint. Lee, who was experiencing something of a midlife crisis and had been planning on leaving the company, decided to go out on a high note, writing a comic to his liking that wouldn't condescend to readers.

"I figured the Fantastic Four would be my swan song," Lee said. "I had no idea it would catch on the way it did."

Co-created with Jack Kirby, who had returned to the fold, *The Fantastic Four* followed a team of astronauts—Reed Richards (Mr. Fantastic), Sue Storm (the Invisible Girl), Johnny Storm (the Human Torch) and Ben Grimm (the Thing)—who gain powers after being exposed to cosmic rays, fighting villains as they bicker, a new concept for comic-book "heroes."

The Fantastic Four's success gave rise to more radiation-and-monster-based heroes, with the help of artist Steve Ditko. For Lee this was an intense and fruitful time, as his wife, Joan, recalled to *EW* in 2003. "The characters just ran through Stan's mind like crazy, one after the other," she said. "It was a fantastic period."

Those characters included the Hulk, a Dr. Jekyll/Mr. Hyde antihero struck by gamma rays; Ant-Man, whose size-changing powers resulted from a risky experiment; Spider-Man, a kid bitten by a radioactive spider; and Daredevil, a hero blinded by radioactive bars that fell off a truck.

Some of these heroes went up against the communist menace, an easy villain for instant motivation. Thor, created shortly after the Hulk, became a prisoner in a communist prison in his fifth issue, while Iron Man, created shortly after Ant-Man, faced a variety of Russian and communist Chinese adversaries in his early adventures.

With this lineup proving popular, Atlas finally had its own version of the Justice League and released the first issue of *The Avengers* in 1963. The Avengers bickered too, with members leaving and joining regularly. With the company headed in a bold new direction, Lee persuaded Goodman to change its name to Marvel.

The difference in styles between the two big comics publishers was striking: DC's heroes leveraged their powers to help others and eagerly teamed up; Marvel heroes bemoaned their complicated lives and mistrusted one another. These two universes dominated this silver age of comics, following the original 1940s golden age.

Marvel's ascendancy was all thanks to Lee, who believed readers wanted heroes they could both look up to and relate to. These weren't glossy do-gooders who never made mistakes—they were men and women with heart and humanity. Their appeal was undeniable.

"There must have been something in the air at that time," Lee recalled. "It was like I couldn't do anything wrong."

The same year that the Avengers finally assembled, Marvel, with Lee still at the helm as editor in chief, introduced a whole new breed of superhero. Led by wheelchair-user Charles Xavier (Professor X), the X-Men included Beast (Hank McCoy), Iceman (Bobby Drake), Marvel Girl (Jean Grey), Angel (Warren Worthington III) and Cyclops (Scott Summers). These X-Men were heroes whose powers came not from outer space but from within their very DNA. *The X-Men* #1 hit shelves in September 1963.

Presented "In the Sensational Fantastic Four Style!" (as the cover trumpeted), these heroes weren't that much older than their core readership. They were mutants. People—kids, really—whose very chromosomal makeup had evolved them beyond normal humankind. Like the millions of disenfranchised youngsters who read

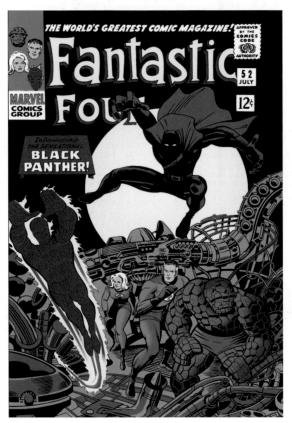

◄
Black Panther (aka T'Challa) made his Marvel debut in *Fantastic Four* #52. The 1966 introduction of the superhero and his technologically advanced African nation of Wakanda— during the midst of the civil rights movement— was highly progressive for the medium, but Lee and his artists knew it was important for readers to see themselves reflected in comics.

comic books, these heroic reader stand-ins were outcasts, subjected to hatred and ridicule because of something they couldn't control. If readers were discounted by society because they were a member of a minority (racial or sexual), a nerd or even a girl(!), the heroes were similarly challenged because of their color, abilities or size. The X-Men weren't just like their readers, they were their readers. It was a savvy approach given the unrest in the country and the burgeoning civil rights and women's liberation movements.

By the mid-'60s, Lee could have hung up his pencil, having already solidified his bona fides as a titan of the industry.

"Stan is up there with Walt Disney and George Lucas," said writer-director Kevin Smith to *EW*. "The man's created—or

co-created, as he's always quick to point out—so many characters that have defined superheroics and comics over the last 50-plus years, he should be ensconced in that pantheon of great American creators whose art has left an indelible mark on not just our culture but the world."

### GROWING PAINS

Despite the imprint's runaway success in the early to mid-'60s, Marvel's halcyon days wouldn't last. Changes were afoot. In 1966 Steve Ditko, the artist who drew Spider-Man and Doctor Strange (and co-created Spider-Man with Lee), quit. Then four years later Kirby defected to DC Comics, a dramatic event given that his partnership with Lee had forged some of the most iconic comics characters of all time. Kirby would

# COMICS AS POLITICAL COMMENTARY

Chadwick Boseman's T'Challa fights Erik Killmonger (Michael B. Jordan) for the crown in 2018's *Black Panther.*

Though they're often dismissed as juvenilia, superhero comics have been political since their beginnings—Superman was pro-labor, Batman believed in vigilante justice, and Captain America punched Nazis. Subtle sentiments often seemed to seep, almost helplessly, into the pages, or sneak by the bottom-line-watching editors. When Marvel introduced its first superhero of color, the Black Panther, in 1966, Stan Lee didn't realize the ramifications of the name. Marvel briefly tried to put distance between the superhero and Huey Newton's Black Panther party by renaming its character Black Leopard and by giving him dialogue like "I neither condemn nor condone those who have taken up the name." By the end of the 1960s, though, it had become commercially unviable to not take an occasional stand on issues, and since then, the genre has provided generations of agitating writers with a soapbox. Here's how Lee and Marvel got their message across:

**FANTASTIC FOUR #52,** *1966*
Black Panther—otherwise known as T'Challa, king of the fictional African country of Wakanda—made his debut alongside the supersquad, becoming the first mainstream comic-book character of African descent. "I have always included minority characters in my stories, often as heroes," Lee once said. "We live in a diverse society—in fact, a diverse world—and we must learn to live in peace and with respect for each other."

**X-MEN: GOD LOVES, MAN KILLS,** *1982*
Since the X-Men's debut in 1963, the nonviolence-preaching Professor Xavier and the militant Magneto have occasionally brought to mind the respective philosophies of Martin Luther King Jr. and Malcolm X, but this 1982 graphic novel about a mutant-hating televangelist made the civil rights metaphors explicit. (Pat Robertson's *700 Club* soon after devoted airtime to denouncing it.)

**MARVEL BOY,** *2000*
More than a decade before the 2011 Occupy Wall Street movement, there were WTO riots, the activist Naomi Klein and Grant Morrison's Marvel Boy, who fought a sentient corporation in the streets of New York City ("It's marketing the planet as its own, warning off other celestial predators!"). Artist J.G. Jones stocked the background with ironic product placements of Teletubbies, Sony and Batman.

**CIVIL WAR,** *2006*
The U.S. government responds to an incident of mass destruction in suburban Connecticut caused by an exploding supervillain—by passing the Superhuman Registration Act (yes, this was in the wake of the 2001 Patriot Act), leading to a rift between those supporting heightened security (such as Iron Man) and those supporting civil liberties (such as Captain America, who ended up dead…for a while). —**SEAN HOWE**

return in 1975, but things would never be quite the same, and in 1979 he left for good. Lee's position at Marvel also changed in the '70s, as he transitioned from the position of editor to that of publisher (he also served as president for a brief time). And by the 1990s Lee had all but stepped away from his formal duties at Marvel.

In early 1992 Marvel suffered another staffing crisis when seven of its top artists—Todd McFarlane (*Spider-Man*), Jim Lee (*X-Men*), Rob Liefeld (*X-Force*), Marc Silvestri (*Wolverine*), Erik Larsen (*The Amazing Spider-Man*), Jim Valentino (*Guardians of the Galaxy*) and Whilce Portacio (*The Uncanny X-Men*)—left to form their own imprint, Image Comics.

With the comic-book industry flagging by the mid-'90s—as a result of, at least in part, the emergence of the World Wide Web—Marvel's parent company, Marvel Entertainment Group, filed for Chapter 11 bankruptcy protection.

Yet by the late '90s a turnaround was in sight. The 1998 movie *Blade*, starring Wesley Snipes as a vampire killer, became the first successful film based on a Marvel character. That same year, Marvel emerged from bankruptcy, regained the film rights to *Spider-Man* (which had been pinballing around since 1985) and promptly resold them to Sony. Marvel also welcomed Lee back into the fold, awarding him the title of chairman emeritus in perpetuity, which came with an annual salary of $1 million.

The bigger comics publishers began to poach talent from the smaller ones. Marvel hired Event Comics' Joe Quesada and Jimmy Palmiotti to run the second-tier Marvel Knights imprint; that team brought in such creators as Kevin Smith and the then-unknown Brian Michael Bendis, and two years later Quesada stepped into the role of Marvel's editor in chief. DC bought Jim Lee's Image imprint WildStorm, which launched Alan Moore's America's Best Comics line (and most notably the Victorian superteam the League of Extraordinary Gentlemen) and Warren Ellis and Bryan Hitch's grand, brutal, wildly influential series *The Authority*.

By the end of the decade, with the

◄ Billed "The Strangest Super-Heroes of All!" the X-Men broke onto the scene in 1963. Another timely creation from Marvel, the mutant squad illustrated that it was okay to be different at a time when individuality wasn't prized.

dot-com boom in full swing and *Batman Beyond* the only animated show with more than a few episodes left to run, superheroes were almost entirely the province of comic books—and only a few of those managed to crack the important 100,000 sales mark each month. But there was a huge change coming in the form of a movie that appeared in the summer of 2000, based on a series whose film rights Marvel had sold seven years earlier to 20th Century Fox: *X-Men*.

## SILVER-SCREEN SENSATIONS

Superheroes were, of course, no strangers to screens big and small during the 20th century. Superman leapt onto TV screens in 1952 with the debut of *Adventures of Superman*, and Batman followed 14 years

later. Both would become matinee idols, with Richard Donner's big-screen film *Superman* in 1978 and Tim Burton's *Batman* in 1989. But while DC was finding some purchase leveraging its biggest names, Marvel couldn't keep up. Lee had long lobbied to get the superheroes he created onto movie screens—often to no avail. That changed with the 2000 release of Bryan Singer's *X-Men*, which became a surprise smash hit and finally convinced Hollywood once and for all that audiences really did want to see superheroes.

The surprise success turned into a genuine phenomenon in 2002, when Sam Raimi's *Spider-Man* was released to record-breaking ticket sales. The floodgates were open. *Spider-Man*, unlike *X-Men*, was entirely unabashed in its embrace of what

# 'MUTANT' AS CODE WORD

Alan Cumming stars as Nightcrawler in 2003's *X2: X-Men United.*

I n a 2004 interview with the Television Academy Foundation's Archive of American Television, Stan Lee was matter-of-fact about the root of his characters' powers. He attributed the source of the X-Men's abilities to their simply being "born that way"—this was about seven years before Lady Gaga's similarly named anthem to individuality would hit the airwaves. And this declaration is all the evidence you need that attitudes toward being different were, well, different than they had been in the 1960s.

Code words, weighted with innuendo and not-necessarily-silent judgment, were and are still used in polite society to veil the homophobia, racism, xenophobia and misogyny ingrained in the literal and figurative social conversation. The meaning was clear when you called someone's brother "theatrical," a spinster aunt "independent," a little-seen uncle "special" or the new woman your grandmother hired to clean her house "girl." All people persecuted (and prosecuted) for their very nature. Them. Others. Freaks. Outcasts. *Mutants.*

By claiming, if not celebrating, the word "mutant," *X-Men* comic books, which debuted in 1963, were a salve for readers who looked toward pop culture for characters like themselves. In a time when the buttoned-down Don Draper aesthetic was the all-American ideal, the bald and wheelchair-using Charles Xavier was positioned as a respected and all-powerful father figure. He trained his students to fight evil, but more important, he created a safe space. Xavier's School for Gifted Youngsters took in students—especially those whose parents had abandoned them because of their powers—and made them part of a nurturing, loving environment (admittedly one with a secret arsenal and war room). Anyone and everyone—male (Cyclops), female (Jean Grey), white (Iceman), black (Storm), Asian (Sunfire), blue (Beast), Jewish (Shadowcat), Catholic (Nightcrawler), rich (Angel) or poor (Gambit)—could come together and live their truth in a judgment-free, welcoming environment led by someone who could sympathize and empathize with their individuality.

The X-Men never shied away from what was, and remains, the most obvious mutant-as-code trope. In 1979 *X-Men* #120 introduced Northstar, who would go on to become the first openly gay superhero in a mainstream comic book, and in 2015 original X-Men team member Iceman, who exists in modern times as both his younger and older self (it's a long story), was outed as gay by Jean Grey (it's a long story). One wonders what young Jean's reaction would have been 50 years ago, but today she knows he was just born that way.

**—ROBB PEARLMAN**

comic-book characters looked and felt like: While you could get away with characterizing *X-Men* as a science-fiction film, *Spider-Man* was 100 percent comic book—joyous, colorful and utterly charming.

With the two movies' boffo box office, Lee pursued a cut of the profits, as he believed his contract with Marvel entitled him to 10 percent. He filed suit in Manhattan federal court in November 2002, telling *EW*, "I'm hoping my lawsuit will go down as the friendliest lawsuit in history. I love the guys at Marvel, I love the company, I love the spirit and the potential." (Marvel eventually settled with Lee in 2005 for an undisclosed amount.) Lee would continue his role as the friendly face of the brand, making Comic-Con appearances and showing up in cheeky movie cameos ("I don't really see a need to retire as long as I am having fun," he said in 2006 when he was 83), and the company would continue to churn out films.

In fact, after *Spider-Man*, it was open season for Marvel characters—studios that had been sitting on film rights suddenly made good on them: There was *Daredevil* and *Hulk* and *The Punisher,* among others, while across company lines DC played small ball with movies like *Catwoman* and *Constantine,* and more obscure comics from publishers outside of the big two got a shot at blockbuster fame with the likes of *Hellboy.* In 2005 Warner Bros. decided it was time for DC's biggest superhero to make a comeback, choosing auteur Christopher Nolan to reboot Batman in *Batman Begins.*

Thanks to *X-Men* and the films that followed, superhero movies had breadth. *Batman Begins* (2005) gave them depth. *Begins* was a film less interested in bringing a comic book to the screen than in delving into the reasons a comic-book character mattered, plumbing the psyches of its characters against the backdrop of a thrilling plot—with an ensemble full of award-winning actors to boot. It was a thesis statement, a declaration that we hadn't been using superheroes to the extent that we could.

*Iron Man,* which followed shortly in 2008, marked the latest step in the

▲
Recognize that hunk of metal? It's Iron Man (aka Tony Stark) in his first issue, dating back to 1963. Lee liked the idea of creating a character whose lifestyle and beliefs—a billionaire military contractor!—contradicted and challenged readers' own. Ironically, Iron Man would become one of Lee's most beloved creations.

evolution of superhero movies. Jon Favreau's film suggested that there were other superheroes out there, and we would see them onscreen—first individually (*The Incredible Hulk, Thor, Captain America, Black Panther*) and then all together (*The Avengers*). Superhero movies were finally like superhero comics, not works isolated from one another but part of a wider tapestry. What's more, this tapestry was woven out of characters Marvel had not yet licensed to other studios, which allowed Marvel to place its branding front and center and become a household name—one that Disney would buy for $4 billion in 2009.

The rules are different now: Marvel proved that audiences are interested in sprawling cinematic stories that are bigger than any one character. Lee's vision for a cinematic universe featuring Earth's Mightiest Heroes—the men and women he so brilliantly brought to life during his decades at Marvel—has been realized. And while he wasn't present to see the conclusion of Phase Three with the 2019 premiere of *Avengers: Endgame,* Lee helped set a course for Marvel—and for the comics industry at large—that shows no sign of stopping anytime soon.

"Stan created a whole new set of superheroes," said author Tom Wolfe in 1972. "In fact, I'd say he put 'superhero' into the language. Superman did it first, but Stan brought the breed to maturity."

*By Nancy Lambert, John Jackson Miller, Robb Pearlman, Joshua Rivera, Tom Sinclair, Oliver Sava, Craig Shutt, Amy Wilkinson and Douglas Wolk*

# IRON MAN MEETS THE...
# STARK REALITY

Robert Downey Jr. stars as the billionaire-turned-superhero Tony Stark in 2013's *Iron Man 3*.

**W**ith Tony Stark (aka Iron Man), Stan Lee created a character who would challenge readers of the 1960s. "I think I gave myself a dare," Lee recalled in 2008. "It was the height of the Cold War. The readers, the young readers, if there was one thing they hated, it was war, it was the military....So I got a hero who represented that to the hundredth degree. He was a weapons manufacturer, he was providing weapons for the Army, he was rich, he was an industrialist....I thought it would be fun to take the kind of character that nobody would like and shove him down their throats and make them like him....And he became very popular."

Popular—and always at the center of the cultural conversation.

## POLITICAL UNDERPINNINGS

Tony Stark's superhero career began in 1963 in Vietnam, before most Americans knew its location. Wounded by a land mine, Stark used American ingenuity—and the help of fellow prisoner Professor Ho Yinsen—to save his life with a super-suit, then rescued locals from a bullying warlord. His creativity, patriotism and roguish autonomy informed many of his stories, as America's enemies became his own. His origin has been updated to the Persian Gulf and later Afghanistan.

## BATTLING THE RED SCARE

Iron Man was the Marvel Universe's foremost weapon in the battle against communism. In his fourth issue he fought the Red Barbarian, a communist spy leader whose colorful name referred to his politics, unlike those of most supervillains. Stark also fought Russia's Crimson Dynamo, who defected. That led to visits from a replacement Dynamo, Natasha Romanoff (aka the Black Widow) and Titanium Man.

## GOVERNMENTAL RELATIONS

Stark's autonomy made legislators nervous. They subpoenaed him to testify before Congress in the mid-1960s (but he got out of it). Through the years he invented many of S.H.I.E.L.D.'s coolest weapons but transitioned from munitions to technology innovations. He worked with (or resisted) military officials as times changed. After 9/11 he served a stint as Secretary of Defense.

—**CRAIG SHUTT**

150 —

# The Author, Measured

Stan Lee was Marvel Comics' top editor for nearly 30 years (until 1972). During that time he co-created some of the most iconic characters of all time, including Spider-Man, the Fantastic Four and the Hulk. But as it turns out, his longest-running author credits occurred on comics you've probably never heard of. *EW*'s Tim Leong looks at the longevity of some comics you recognize—and some you don't (hello, Millie the Model!)—in this infographic from his 2013 book *Super Graphic: A Visual Guide to the Comic Book Universe,* published by Chronicle Books.

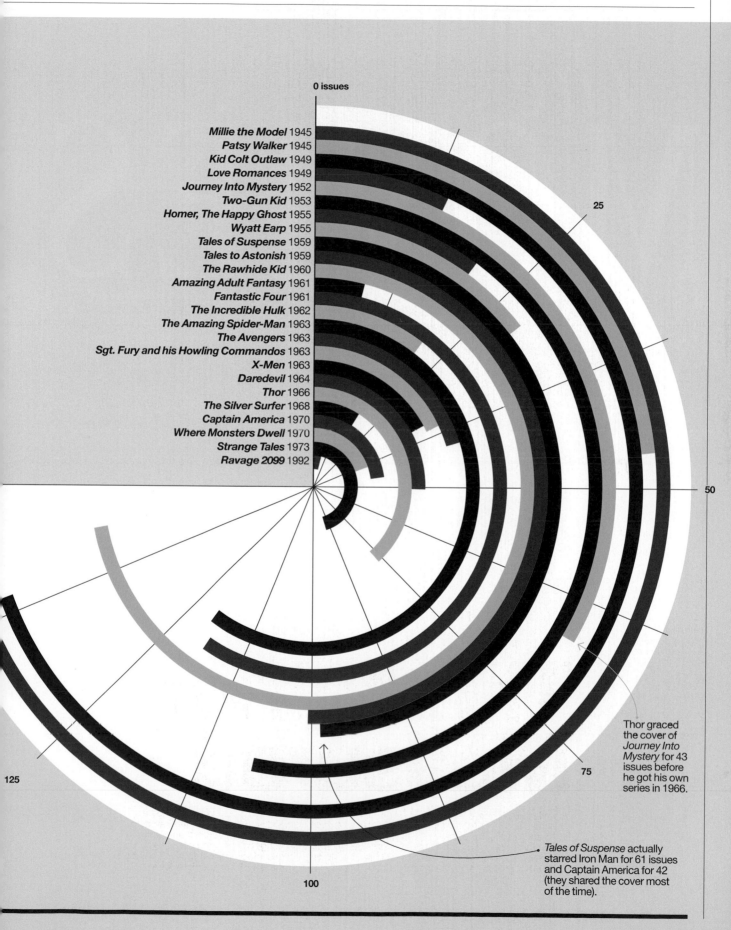

0 issues

25

50

75

100

125

*Millie the Model* 1945
*Patsy Walker* 1945
*Kid Colt Outlaw* 1949
*Love Romances* 1949
*Journey Into Mystery* 1952
*Two-Gun Kid* 1953
*Homer, The Happy Ghost* 1955
*Wyatt Earp* 1955
*Tales of Suspense* 1959
*Tales to Astonish* 1959
*The Rawhide Kid* 1960
*Amazing Adult Fantasy* 1961
*Fantastic Four* 1961
*The Incredible Hulk* 1962
*The Amazing Spider-Man* 1963
*The Avengers* 1963
*Sgt. Fury and his Howling Commandos* 1963
*X-Men* 1963
*Daredevil* 1964
*Thor* 1966
*The Silver Surfer* 1968
*Captain America* 1970
*Where Monsters Dwell* 1970
*Strange Tales* 1973
*Ravage 2099* 1992

Thor graced the cover of *Journey Into Mystery* for 43 issues before he got his own series in 1966.

*Tales of Suspense* actually starred Iron Man for 61 issues and Captain America for 42 (they shared the cover most of the time).

# the
# MOVIES

As his outsize characters exploded onto the big screen, Stan Lee kept busy. He started a media production company, set up a foundation to promote literacy, visited dozens of conventions to meet with fans firsthand and still made cameos in more than 30 films

In one of his many movie appearances, Lee played a mailman in 2005's *Fantastic Four*.

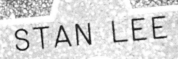

# The Face of Marvel

*EW'S* **ANTHONY BREZNICAN** BIDS FAREWELL TO THE MAN WHO KNEW THAT HEARTACHE AND HUMANITY MADE A HERO STRONGER

**AS FANS THE WORLD OVER MOURNED THE** passing of Stan Lee, I was reminded of meeting him for the first time many years ago and hearing the astounding true story of Marvel's mightiest heroes from "Stan the Man" himself.

It was April 2002, and we were sitting in the Santa Monica offices of his new company POW! Entertainment—except Lee wasn't really sitting. He was up and antic, slinging his hand out in the Spider-Man pose and telling war stories of a battle with Green Goblin. Even at age 79, he was practically crawling up the walls himself.

The first Tobey Maguire webslinger movie was set to debut in a few weeks, and hopes for its success were Empire State Building-high after 2000's *X-Men* proved to studios that comic-book movies were

◄
In January 2011 Stan Lee received a star on the Hollywood Walk of Fame.

maybe, kinda something audiences were excited to see.

Remember, this was six years before *Iron Man* and the launch of the Marvel Cinematic Universe. The films were not yet interconnected, not that there were many to string together. Stan Lee cameos were not yet a phenomenon. He had played a beachside hot-dog vendor in the *X-Men* film. ("You missed me?" he teased. "I was like the lead of the movie!")

A crowd scene in Sam Raimi's *Spider-Man* would be one of his first "Stan Lee appearances," but when I sat down to interview him for the Associated Press, he was a little worried because he'd seen a rough cut of the film already, and his sequence had been shortened.

"The [original] idea was, I was selling sunglasses in Times Square and I was talking to this little girl, showing her a pair of glasses as Peter Parker walks by," Lee recounted in his gruff, nasal voice. "So I reach out to Peter Parker and say, 'Would you like a pair of these? They're the kind of sunglasses they wore in *X-Men!*'"

He clapped his hands and rocked in his chair, a big grin spreading beneath his salt-and-peppery mustache. "It would have gotten the biggest laugh! But they cut it out because the film ran a little long."

He shrugged. He still made the final cut, and Raimi included one of the changes that Lee suggested. After creating so many heroes, Lee wanted to play one himself. "The Green Goblin drops a bomb, and we all ran," Lee said. "After he shot it, I said, 'Sam, that isn't right. I shouldn't leave that poor little girl and go running for my life. I'm going to carry her with me.'"

## A HERO . . . STUMBLES

On the next take of the scene, Raimi gave him the go-ahead. But there was another problem: She may have only been a little kid, but he was a skinny old guy. "I tried to lift her and tried to lift her, and I couldn't!" Lee cackled. "She was only a little girl, but she must have weighed 500 lbs."

He ended up grabbing her hand and leading her away instead. (In *Spider-Man 2*

he turned up to do a similar task as a man who pulls a woman away from a chunk of falling concrete.)

"Ang Lee is doing the Hulk," he said. "There's a scene for me, so I'll go to San Francisco and make a fool of myself again. Another guy is doing a Daredevil movie."

Lee sighed. He crossed his arms in his mustard-colored cardigan and shrugged. How long would this superhero-movie thing last? He didn't know. He was glad to be along for the ride. Happy to see the old characters he helped create being brought to life onscreen.

We began talking about the origin of Spider-Man, born in 1962 after a string of other successes had made Stan Lee a powerhouse scribe at Marvel Comics.

He had started working there when he

was a teenager. Back then Marvel Comics was Timely Comics, and he was known as Stanley Lieber, son of Jewish Romanian immigrants from the Bronx. His dream was to become a writer. A novelist, maybe.

But before any of that could happen, he earned cash by working a series of small jobs. His first claim to fame as a theater usher was tripping and falling while showing Eleanor Roosevelt to her seat. ("Are you all right, young man?" she asked.) He also delivered sandwiches for a drugstore and became an office assistant at, in his words, "the world's second-largest trouser manufacturer."

His writing career began with obituaries. Many of them were about famous people, and he was required to prepare them in advance so newspapers could

rush them into print when the celebrity died. "I got depressed writing about living people in the past tense," Lee told me.

He didn't want to write about death. He wanted to write about things that were larger than life.

## THE BIRTH OF SPIDEY

Lee's big break came when his cousin-in-law Martin Goodman hired him to work at Timely, writing westerns, love stories and comedy cartoons.

"When I got into comics, nobody, nobody, had any respect for them," he told me. "Even most of the people in the field were embarrassed. It was no job for a grown man, doing these silly comics that other people looked down their noses at."

That's why he created a pen name by cutting his first name in half. Decades later he described it as his biggest regret.

"My name was Stanley Martin Lieber," he said, his outstretched hand marking the syllables in the air. "A real legitimate name—with a lilt! I used to write it out as a kid all the time and think how good that would look on the Declaration of Independence. I always thought I'd be a really good writer someday."

Superheroes weren't part of the funny-book zeitgeist at that point, although Batman and Superman at DC Comics changed that. Goodman came to "Stan Lee" and asked for ideas.

Instead of the loner hero, Lee proposed a family of heroes—and the Fantastic Four were born. Then he thought he would take a villainous character—a monster—and make that the hero. The Incredible Hulk smashed his way into pop-culture history.

"When you try to create a new superhero, you have to keep creating a superpower that's different," he said. "With Hulk I had the strongest living human being. I thought, 'What's left?' While I was thinking, I saw a fly crawling on the wall and I thought, 'That would be cool!...The next thing I needed was a name. Crawl-Man? Nah, that didn't have it. Insect-Man? I ran down the list. Mosquito-Man, Beetle-Man, Fly-Man. Then I hit on...Spider-Man."

With those words, Lee's hands flashed in the air. His eyebrows shot up.

"It somehow had a dramatic feeling, a scary feeling," he said. "I thought, 'That's it!' And lo, a legend was born."

## CREDIT WHERE DUE

One of the controversies surrounding Lee was how much credit he actually deserved. Many of "his" characters were crafted in concert with artists like Jack Kirby, who would take Lee's concept and run with it.

Whether Lee grabbed more credit than he deserved or merely attracted the attention by way of his natural showmanship as an extrovert among a team of introverts, I never found him to be anything except generous with praise for his artists. When we spoke, Lee himself went out of his way to shout out his early chief Spider-Man collaborator, Steve Ditko, who died in June 2018 at age 90.

"I try to share the responsibility," Lee said. "Steve is the guy who designed Spider-Man and gave Spider-Man so much of that eerie spidery feeling. Later he helped with the plots and did the plots." Lee beamed his signature smile again: "Steve has to share the blame as well as me."

The key to Spider-Man, he revealed, was failure. Peter Parker was a weakling, a teenager, and he wasn't on a mission of revenge—he was fueled by regret because he already had his power and failed to stop the crook who would go on to kill his beloved uncle Ben.

"With great power comes great responsibility" was a lesson that haunted him

▲
Fans swarmed Lee at Comic-Con San Diego in 2007.

▶
While filming his cameo in *Fantastic Four: Rise of the Silver Surfer,* Lee chatted with director Tim Story in 2007.

because he learned it too late.

"The most important thing is to make the reader care and sympathize with a character," Lee said. "The more problems a character has and the more unhappy and troubled he is, it makes that person seem human to [the readers]."

## EVEN MORE FAILURE

Spider-Man is perhaps Lee's most renowned creation...which is why it's ironic that no one initially liked his idea about the kid who becomes a webslinger after being bitten by a radioactive spider.

"I was told in chapter and verse by the fellow who was then my publisher that it was the worst idea he'd ever heard," Lee said. "'People hate spiders! You can't call a hero Spider-Man!...Stan, don't you understand that teenagers can only be sidekicks?'"

Lee had stumbled onto the idea of representation—the young readers of comic books may like to see a hero who looks like themselves. It would be a lesson that led him later to co-create the first black superhero—the Wakandan warrior king Black Panther—as well as the first African-American hero, the high-flying Falcon.

After absorbing all the Spider-Man criticism, Lee delivered more bad news to Goodman. "When I told him that I wanted Peter Parker to have a lot of problems and worries and be unsure of himself, he said, 'Ugh! It's obvious you have no conception of what a hero really is!'"

The thing that saved Spider-Man's life

The stars of 2005's *Fantastic Four* (from left to right): Chris Evans, Michael Chiklis, Lee in his cameo outfit, Jessica Alba and Ioan Gruffudd.

was the death of one of the brands. "We were killing that magazine, much as I loved it," Lee said. "We tried to do *Amazing Adult Fantasy* as *The Twilight Zone*." But it hadn't succeeded.

"When you're doing the last issue of a magazine you're about to kill, nobody really cares what you put in it. So I figured I'd get Spider-Man out of my system." Lee and Ditko worked on the story together, and Kirby did the dramatic lead image of Spidey swinging through the streets of Manhattan holding a crook at his side.

"We put him on the cover and forgot about him," Lee said. "Then a couple months later, when sales figures came in, the publisher came to me and said, 'Stan, you remember that character that we both liked?'" The Stan Lee smile propped up that mustache again. "'That Spider-Man of yours…? Why don't we make a series out of him?'"

## FINDING HUMANITY IN MUTANTS

After 100 issues of *The Amazing Spider-Man,* Lee said, he turned over the writing to Roy Thomas. By that point, he had too many characters to juggle without a large team. "It was hard, of course, but I was letting go of all the characters at the same time—there was the Hulk, Doctor Strange, the Avengers, Iron Man, Daredevil, the X-Men. After that I got kinda used to it," Lee said.

One of his proudest collaborations was the X-Men, which resulted in part because Lee had exhausted seemingly every possible excuse for how a human being could develop superpowers.

Weary of radioactive insects, toxic spills and gamma-ray bursts, he came up with a shortcut: They were simply mutants, born that way. It gave the X-Men a surprising power in the real world as a metaphor for civil rights of all kinds.

"To keep it realistic, I knew most people dislike and distrust those who are different from them," Lee said. "I thought maybe we could even get a little moral lesson in this thing. Here are people who are good, who are trying to help humanity, and the very humans they are trying to help are hunting them and hounding them and harassing them."

Lee's own superpower was not just his imagination but also his ability to create things that others could run with and make their own. His characters endure because, like the Fantastic Four's Reed Richards, they're able to be stretched and changed to fit new writers and times.

Lee became the face of Marvel, the wisecracking "Stan the Man" who talked to kids in their own language ("'Nuff said") without talking down to them. In his "Stan's Soapbox" column, he often advocated for fairness and kindness to everyone—a grown-up message delivered via the funny papers.

Strangely enough, Lee said he would cast himself as the opposite of all that in his own imagination, drawing a comparison to the cynical, uncompromising newspaper editor J. Jonah Jameson. "I'm very frustrated that by the time they made the movie, I was too old to play the role," Lee said. "I modeled him after me. He was dumb and loudmouthed and opinionated. He was me."

Of all the characters he helped create, Peter Parker remained his favorite.

## A FAVORITE SON

"In a way Spider-Man is more special than the others," he said.

"Nothing ever goes right for Peter. I think for most people in the world, nothing ever goes right. He has his share of mistakes and his share of problems as he

▲
Lee at the premiere of *Ant-Man* in Hollywood in 2015.

▶
Marc Webb, the director of *The Amazing Spider-Man 2,* leaning in to consult with Lee.

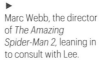

goes through life."

Peter Parker also never gives up, a trait he shares with his originator.

"People always ask me, 'Why don't you retire?' When you retire, what do you do? You say, 'At last I can do all the things I've always wanted to do.' But I'm already doing the things I always wanted to do!" Lee said.

He had a child who died in infancy and one grown daughter, an artist, with his wife, Joan, who died just last year in 2017, also at age 95. Back in 2002 he said that she was his fun. "When I go home, I love being with my wife. I love watching television. I love sitting at the computer and coming up with whatever I come up with. Hobby is my work."

Even after leaving Marvel and pursuing assorted other ventures, Lee remained the public face of the comic-book company—as iconic as any of its heroes—and his presence as a Marvel ambassador and cameo king was a reminder that larger-than-life heroes we love are simply a representation of the ideals of a puny human (or team of humans).

He relished his newfound fame as a star. "I'm one of the top cameo actors," he said. "If you don't blink, you'll see me running fearfully for my life."

Apart from changing his name so long ago, and never writing that Great American Novel, Lee had only one other regret:

"I wish there was a cameo category in the Academy Awards."

▲
Behind the scenes
and on the set of
2002's *Spider-Man,*
Lee with producer
Avi Arad.

❝In a way, Spider-Man is more
special than the others. Nothing
ever goes right for Peter. I think
for most people in the world,
nothing ever goes right❞
—STAN LEE

**MARVEL'S AGENT CARTER, 2015**
For a season 1 episode entitled "The Blitzkrieg Button," Stan Lee appeared as a shoeshine patron who bums the sports section off of Dominic Cooper's Howard Stark. (Yes, that's him behind the broadsheet!)

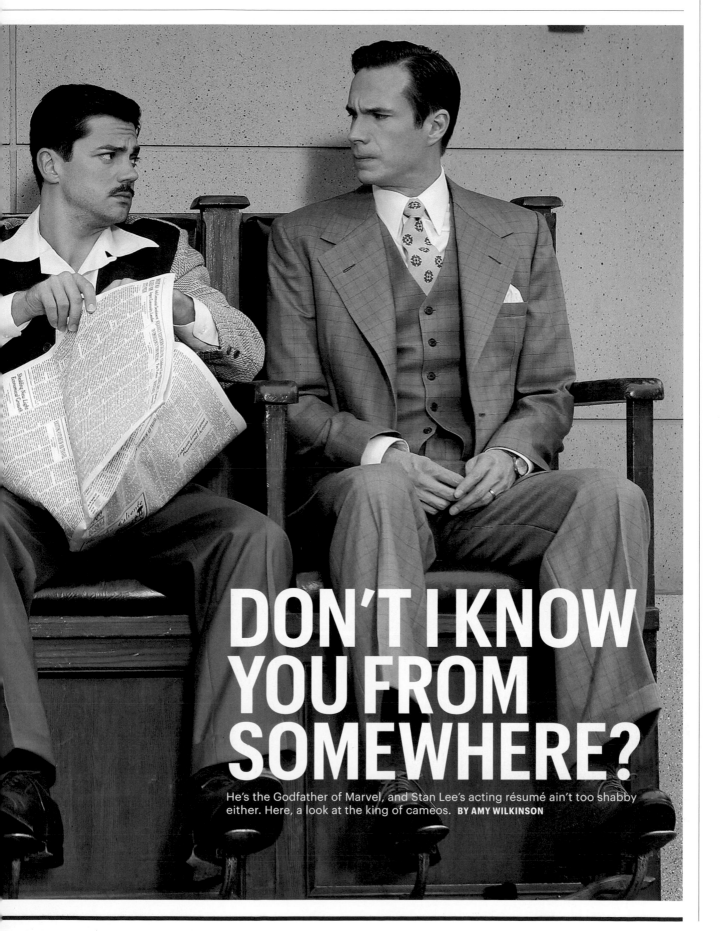

# DON'T I KNOW YOU FROM SOMEWHERE?

He's the Godfather of Marvel, and Stan Lee's acting résumé ain't too shabby either. Here, a look at the king of cameos. **BY AMY WILKINSON**

▲ **PHINEAS AND FERB, 2013**

And that, boys and girls, is what we call corporate synergy. In 2013 the Disney XD series welcomed Iron Man, Spider-Man, Hulk and Thor in the crossover "Phineas and Ferb: Mission Marvel." Naturally, an animated Lee appeared as a hot-dog vendor.

▶ **ULTIMATE SPIDER-MAN, 2012-16**

Stan Lee really stretched for this Disney XD role, playing a man named...Stan Lee. In a multi-episode arc he guest-starred as a benevolent janitor (and original S.H.I.E.L.D. member) at Peter Parker's high school.

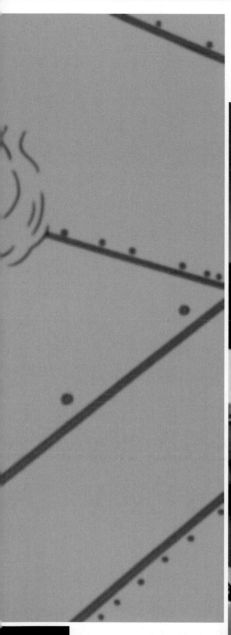

► **HEROES, 2007**

Who's driving the bus? Stan Lee! For the season 1 episode "Unexpected," Lee put on a three-piece suit and got behind the wheel to chauffeur Hiro (Masi Oka).

▶
**MALLRATS, *1995***
Sporting an uncharacteristi-
cally scruffy beard, Lee
appeared as himself in the
stoner flick, dispensing
advice to lovesick teen
Brodie (played by Jason Lee).
Stan Lee would later say that
*Mallrats* was his favorite
movie role of all time.

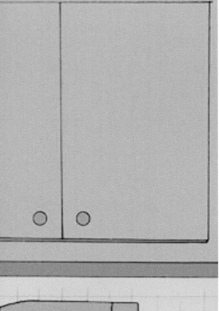

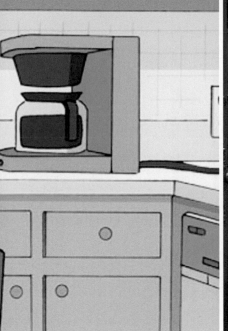

**◄ FAMILY GUY: THE QUEST FOR STUFF, 2014**
Lee—alongside fellow nerd bait Felicia Day, George Takei and Patrick Stewart—appeared in this mobile game set at the fictional Quahog Comic-Con, just in time for that year's real-life San Diego Comic-Con.

**▼ THE BIG BANG THEORY, 2010**
In an episode aptly titled "The Excelsior Acquisition," Lee once again made a cameo as himself—finding Sheldon (Jim Parsons) and Penny (Kaley Cuoco) at his doorstep after they missed a comic-book-store meet and greet. *Excelzinga*?!

❝I got a big kick out of *Mallrats*. But it wasn't a cameo; I really had a role in the movie❞

—STAN LEE

► **FRESH OFF THE BOAT,** *2017*

"It was like a dream come true," *Fresh Off the Boat* writer Daniel Carter told *EW* of Stan the Man's cameo on the ABC sitcom. The episode "Pie vs. Cake" finds Eddie and Emery entering a comic-book contest. So you know what that means...

◄
**THE SIMPSONS, 2014**
Lee made a handful of appearances in Springfield over the years, beginning in 2002 when he showed up at the Android's Dungeon & Baseball Card Shop. Lee wasn't afraid to poke fun at himself (and his long rivalry with DC Comics).

▼
**THE AMAZING SPIDER-MAN 2, 2014**
He could have been any doting grandfather or uncle in the commencement-day crowd. But nope, he was Stan Lee, and he was attending Peter and Gwen's graduation. And when Spider-Man swung in, he cheekily exclaimed, "I think I know that guy!"

❝Talk about somebody who delivers
on every expectation you have.
He was so quick, so smart, so funny.
He was just a delight❞
—*FRESH OFF THE BOAT WRITER JEFF CHLEBUS*

At the premiere of *Captain America: Civil War* in 2016.

*the*
MEM

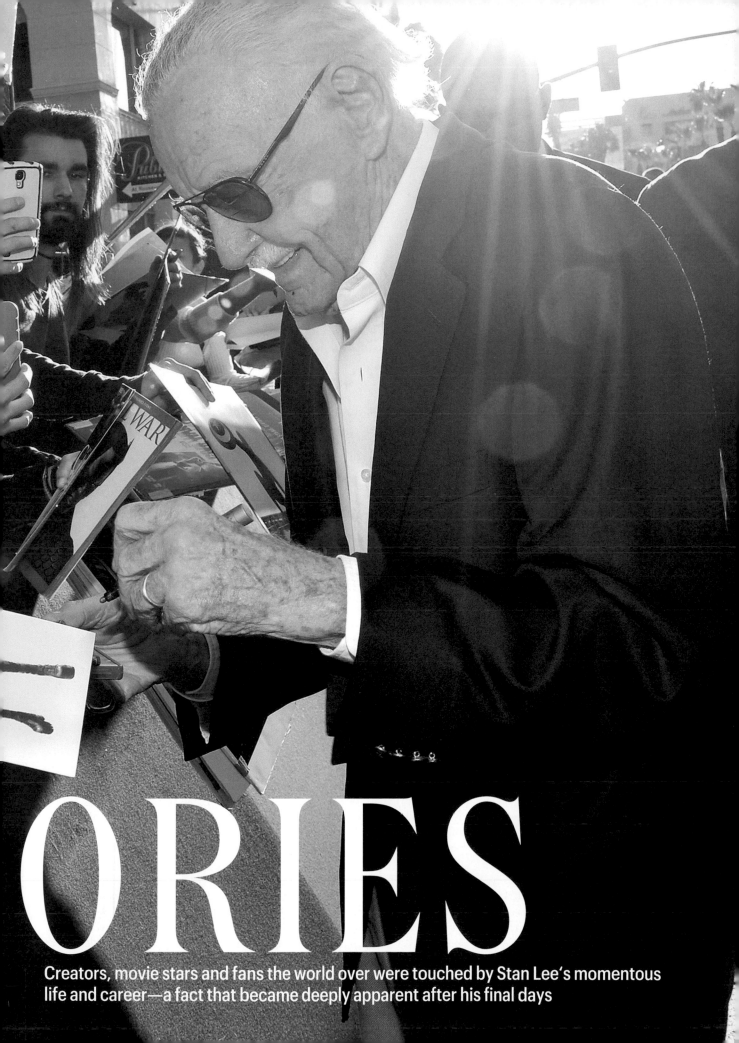

# ORIES

Creators, movie stars and fans the world over were touched by Stan Lee's momentous life and career—a fact that became deeply apparent after his final days

# STAN LEE, TITAN

*Spawn* creator Todd McFarlane recalls a mentor who changed his life when he was just 16—and the industry-reaching impact Lee's genius had on the comic-book genre. **BY CHRISTIAN HOLUB**

Todd McFarlane and Stan Lee in 2017.

**"WHATEVER WE THINK STAN'S LEGACY IS** today, it's just going to keep going, and there's going to be no end," McFarlane tells *EW.* "There's so much that he helped to co-create with his artists. I helped co-create this character Venom, but without Spider-Man there is no Venom. It still all leads back to the '60s comics that Stan and a handful of artists helped create."

"We've seen it with other people who have created some characters and got them to have global impact. Walt Disney was able to create something, and that momentum became so unstoppable that it just keeps expanding. Stan and the people who created those characters with him—we'll look back in 20 years on what people said about his legacy on this day, and we'll think we sold him short. It'll probably be twice as big."

Lee's legacy could even be said to reach beyond Marvel. After making his name on Spider-Man comics, McFarlane eventually left Marvel in the early '90s to cofound a new comics company, Image Comics, alongside fellow superstar artists Jim Lee, Rob Liefeld, Marc Silvestri, Erik Larsen, Jim Valentino and Whilce Portacio. McFarlane and the others had resented editorial interference at Marvel, so they built Image around the idea of creative ownership. To this day Image titles are owned by the writers and artists who created them, not the publisher, which is why it has become home to such beloved and critically acclaimed comics as *The Walking Dead, Saga, Monstress* and more.

Image's focus on creator-owned properties was also inspired by the travails of Marvel creators like Lee, Jack Kirby and Steve Ditko. Since they were on work-for-hire contracts with Marvel, they never reaped the full benefits of the popularity of their creations, such as Spider-Man and the Fantastic Four. Though Lee eventually worked out a deal to become Marvel's "chairman emeritus" with a good share of the profits, it took him years to get as much money out of his own creations as original publisher Martin Goodman did.

"We were inspired both by how Stan and his artists were turning out pages and pages each month so we could enjoy ourselves, and then also by watching them go through the baptism by fire of doing that at a corporation," McFarlane says. "They were the trailblazers for both good and bad. On the creative level it's why we got into the business, and then on the business level it was coming up with a new way of conducting ourselves and our creative community based on what we saw unraveling in front of our eyes. We were the benefactors of knowing where some of the pitfalls were and steered ourselves from places that we knew weren't going to be favorable. I know for a fact if you talk to any of my partners who started the company at that time, they would say the same thing. We were all aware of it and inspired by it."

McFarlane first met Lee as a 16-year-old kid from Canada who had come to Miami to attend baseball camp. The hotel he was staying at also happened to be hosting a comic-book convention. ("Back then, comic conventions could fit in a Holiday Inn ballroom," he says.) At the time, almost every Marvel comic came with the tagline "Stan Lee Presents."

"I saw Stan Lee, and I'm going, 'Oh my gosh!' At this point I have some aspirations of maybe trying to break into comic books. I introduced myself as a fan, like he'd met a thousand times before, and asked, 'Hey, is there any way I can hang out and ask you some questions?' He grabbed a chair, pulled it next to him, tapped it and said, 'Sit down, son,'" McFarlane recalls. "For seven hours I sat there amazed that I was sitting next to Stan Lee. When he wasn't signing signatures, I just

peppered him with questions about everything about comics because I wanted to learn about the industry. Then I went home with a renewed enthusiasm, like, 'I'm going to keep trying to break into this industry!' That was one of those moments that helped lead me not only to breaking into comics, but drawing for Marvel and doing some of the characters Stan created, specifically Spider-Man. The Spider-Man creator on that day did not know the 16-year-old kid sitting next to him would one day draw Spider-Man. And so it came full circle."

"For seven hours I sat there amazed. . . . [Stan Lee] did not know the 16-year-old kid sitting next to him would one day draw Spider-Man"

—TODD McFARLANE

# THE AVENGERS PAY TRIBUTE

Nearly six months after Stan Lee's passing, the actors who had first united in 2012's *The Avengers*, plus Marvel Studios president Kevin Feige, spoke to *EW* about how the comic legend had impacted their lives. **BY ANTHONY BREZNICAN**

**We said goodbye to Stan Lee last year after a big, long life. Do you guys have any poignant memories of him or stories of meeting him from all his Marvel cameos?**

MARK RUFFALO Playing Hulk is like my generation's Hamlet: We're *all* going to get a chance to do it. [*Forced laughter*] So I was really nervous about "Would I please him?" I didn't meet him until the premiere of *The Avengers*. I walked up to him sheepishly, and he's like, "Hey!" and he's like, "You got it, kid!" I was like, "Aww, that's amazing! Thank you, Mr. Lee." Other than Downey and Kevin, I was so nervous over whether he would be happy with what I'd done.

**How about you, Robert, on the first *Iron Man*? Is that when you met Stan Lee for the first time?**

ROBERT DOWNEY JR. Yeah, but my mind goes to *Civil War*, when Rhodey [Don Cheadle's War Machine character] and Tony are having a moment at the end, and [Lee] is playing a FedEx guy. He's like all of us. He's a really big deal, but he's just another schmuck, and we have to get his coverage in the can too. It's like, "And roll sound . . . ," and he's like, "I have a delivery for Tony STANK!" [*Laughter*] It went completely downhill after that. I was like, I am *exactly* like him. It all goes downhill after Take One. You gotta capture it before it's gone.

SCARLETT JOHANSSON Please . . .

DOWNEY You're right, Take Two is my

strong take. But you should stop after that. [*Laughter*] "Aaand . . . he guided it back to himself!"

JOHANSSON I also had a similar moment as Mark when I saw him. I think it was after the *Iron Man 2* premiere, and I was just so nervous. I didn't know how the audience or anybody would react to this beloved character and my interpretation of her, especially because I wasn't originally cast, so I also had a lot of feelings about that. [Emily Blunt had been offered the role first.] I made a career out of that! No. 2! Strong No. 2! [*Laughs*] But yeah, I had a lot of feelings about it, and I saw [Lee] in the theater and he was very excited. I had a big sigh of relief after that.

KEVIN FEIGE The amazing thing is, just as you've all said, he said the *right thing* to the right person at *all* times. Every interaction was what one's dream interaction with Stan Lee would be. He made that come true every single time. He left me a voicemail once in 2004, and I kept it for years until I think the phone disintegrated. It was: "Fearless Feige! Stan Lee here!" I listened to it over and over and over. That's what he was always like. Always supportive.

CHRIS EVANS See, I'm going back to *Fantastic Four*. The first time I met him was 2004, when I was doing Johnny Storm, and the day that he was on-set we actually happened to have a B-roll crew. So one of

my first interactions with him is all caught on [video]. And I found the footage! At the time I was very early in my career, and it was the biggest role I'd ever done. To meet someone like him was so, so overwhelming, and he was in true Stan Lee form—full of life and just so kind and gregarious. He just made me feel right at home.

JEREMY RENNER I aspire to be as strong-

Kevin Feige (far left) and the Avengers assemble onstage during the *Avengers: Endgame* press tour.

minded. The guy lived an amazing life. When you spent time with him, you just knew this guy was burning with the fire of life. He had a great sense of humor and a smart, smart mind. I hope and aspire to be anywhere half of what he was as a man. It's really fantastic.

CHRIS HEMSWORTH He just had a childlike wonder and enthusiasm. You'd want to talk about something like what it all means and so on, and he was just like, "No, I'm just telling stories, and we're having fun!" There's a deeper meaning in the message, which he achieved so beautifully, but the childlike nature about him made me think, "Oh, good, we can all just stay big kids forever." He's the perfect example.

# CELEBRITY MEMORIALS

The mourning for the loss of the Marvel legend continued well past the initial flood of social media posts, first at a star-studded tribute at the TCL Chinese Theatre and then with accolades at the 91st Academy Awards. **BY ALYSSA SMITH**

**IN THE IMMEDIATE WAKE OF THE PASSING OF** Stan Lee, a constellation of stars took to social media to remember the man who had made an indelible impression on their lives. The outpouring of grief came both from actors who had portrayed characters he had created as well as from artists he had inspired for decades.

"Stan Lee was a pioneering force in the superhero universe," wrote Hugh Jackman, whose Wolverine appears in nine films. "I'm proud to have been a small part of his legacy and . . . to have helped bring one of his characters to life."

Newcomer Tom Holland, who portrays the current iteration of Spider-Man, mentioned how indebted he felt to the comic-book creator. "The father of Marvel has made so many people so incredibly happy," he wrote. "What a life and what a thing to have achieved."

Yet Lee's impact stretched far beyond the superheroes he created—he had also inspired a generation of artists, filmmakers and authors to compose their own stories and served as a mentor to many. "When I first broke into Hollywood, he welcomed me with open arms and some very sage advice I'll forever take to heart," wrote Dwayne Johnson. "[Lee was] a true icon who impacted generations around the world."

Those who had worked with the creator for decades, like Marvel television executive Jeph Loeb (*Agents of S.H.I.E.L.D.*),

recalled how inspiring Lee could be. "Stan was just so full of energy and life and had the ability to imbue that in others," said Loeb to *Entertainment Weekly*'s Shirley Li. "For me what Stan will be most remembered for is he taught us all that a hero was the person who stood up when everybody else was told to sit down. He was a huge supporter of the real heroes around us: nurses, doctors, people in the military. He would constantly tell us that the world was filled with heroes." His impact on the comic-book world, from the printed page to television and film, is deeply felt, Loeb says. "Stan changed the game, set the tone for the Marvel Universe, and truly there will never be another one."

*The Avengers* director Joss Whedon echoed the sentiment, sharing a short statement on the social-media platform Twitter. "Stan Lee created a universe where, if a character was beloved enough, they could never really die," Whedon wrote. "Thanks for so much of my life. You'll never not be in it."

Actor and writer Felicia Day also shared memories of Lee. "He was so kind to everyone, especially young artists. He made it seem like your dreams were possible even if you were a misfit. *Especially* if you were a misfit."

It was because of his deep-rooted influence on creators and storytelling that mourning for the creator continued long after Lee's passing. In January, two months

STAN LEE
COMIC BOOK WRITER,
EXECUTIVE PRODUCER

◄ Stan Lee receives
honors at the 91st
Academy Awards.

▼ With Ryan Reynolds
in 2015.

◄ Far left: with Hugh
Jackman in 2008.
Left: with Laura Harrier
and Tom Holland
in 2017.

after Lee's death in mid-November of 2018, a tribute event celebrating the comic-book legend's life took place at the TCL Chinese Theatre in Hollywood. In attendance were hundreds of Marvel fans, colleagues, co-creators, friends and family.

Director Kevin Smith, whose 23-year friendship with Lee began during filming of his 1995 movie *Mallrats,* in which he had written a cameo role for the comics legend, served as a host. In an emotional speech during opening ceremonies, Smith told stories about Stan Lee, Lee's love for the love of his life, his wife, Joanie, and what it meant to him to be able to work so closely with the man.

"A long time ago there was a man born who grew up to tell stories that were the moral foundations of everything I built my life upon, and that's weird, because I was raised Catholic," said Smith in his opening speech. "Stan was a man who told simple stories about the worst thing in the world happening and everyone running away from it. Wisely. Sensibly. But in the midst of that, there was always a handful of people, dressed very colorfully, heading right into it, heading toward danger."

The event also attracted stars like Mark Hamill, Clark Gregg, Seth Green and Felicia Day. During a panel Hamill spoke warmly about the human face Lee had created for Marvel. "He had such a personality that came across the pages.... You really felt like you knew him."

At the event, Laurence Fishburne spoke about how important reading comic books as a teenager was to him and the huge impact it had on his future. "I was in New York City, and they were writing about what was outside the window of New York City. That was so important, because it was really about the place that I was growing up in," said Fishburne. "It opened my mind to the possibility that you could be more than just what your surroundings said that you were supposed to be."

A few weeks later, at the 91st Academy Awards, Stan Lee was honored yet again during the ceremony's "In Memoriam"

▲
Fans in costume surround Kevin Smith (center) as he hosts Excelsior!, an event celebrating the life of Stan Lee, on Jan. 30, 2019, at the TCL Chinese Theatre in Hollywood.

segment, which paid tribute to the late greats in the entertainment industry.

A common thread in all the memorials was how genuine, kind and welcoming Lee was to creators, fans and colleagues alike.

"[Stan Lee] was everything that you hoped he would be. He was everything that you'd dreamed he would be. And he stayed that way, ladies and gentlemen, for 23 years. There was never a moment where I was disappointed by the humanity of Stan Lee, where he let me down," said Smith at the January event. "He was perfection, all the way through."

EXCELSI

ny Life of Stan Lee

A Celebration of the Amazing, Fantastic, Incr

▼

With Mark Hamill
in 2003.

▲

With Joss Whedon
in 2012.

◄

Far left: Felicia Day,
Clark Gregg and
Laurence Fishburne
pay honor to Lee
at Excelsior!
Left: Lee with Dwayne
Johnson in 2017.

# THE FANS IN MOURNING

Celebrities weren't the only ones to remember the comic-book legend. Fans around the world honored the passing of Stan Lee with touching works of their own. **BY AMY WILKINSON**

▶ "I started making comics because of the groundwork Stan Lee laid out. I owe a lot to him," says artist Charlotte Norris.

▲ A remembrance wall emerged at Comic-Con Colombia.

Fans pay tribute to the comic creator.

Spider-Man cosplayers leave flowers at Stan Lee's star on the Hollywood Walk of Fame in Hollywood.

IT WAS SUPPOSED TO BE HALF OF THE UNIVERSE STAN, NOT THE ENTIRE ONE. WOULD YOU MIND ME USING THE TIME STONE ON YOU?... STAN?

STAN LEE
THE CREATOR
1922-2018

So, WHAT DO YOU THINK?

IT'S MORE BEAUTIFUL THAN I COULD HAVE EVER IMAGINED!

BEECHER ARTS

Thor and Lee by Nicholas Beecher.

Thanos, graveside, by Saswata, Susruta and Satadru Mukherjee.

### ENTERTAINMENT WEEKLY
**Editor** Henry Goldblatt
**Executive Editor & Creative Director** Tim Leong

### STAN LEE
**Editorial Director** Kostya Kennedy
**Editors** Alyssa Smith, Amy Wilkinson
**Editor, People + EW Books** Allison Adato
**Art Director** Greg Monfries
**Designers** Sung Choi, Aaron Morales
**Photo Editor** Robert Conway
**Writers** Anthony Breznican, Kevin Feige, Christian Holub,
Sean Howe, Nancy Lambert, Shirley Li, Jeph Loeb,
Todd McFarlane, Kevin Melrose, John Jackson Miller,
Robb Pearlman, Joe Quesada, Joshua Rivera, Rich Sands, Oliver Sava,
Craig Shutt, Tom Sinclair, Kevin Sullivan, Douglas Wolk
**Reporter** Gillian Aldrich, Stewart Allen, Daniel S. Levy, John Wojno
**Copy Desk** Joanann Scali (Chief), James Bradley (Deputy),
Ellen Adamson, Gabrielle Danchick, Richard Donnelly,
Ben Harte, Rose Kaplan, Matt Weingarden
**Production Designer** Peter Niceberg
**Premedia Executive Director** Richard Prue
**Senior Manager** Romeo Cifelli
**Manager** Rob Roszkowski
**Imaging Production Associate** Ana Kaljaj
**Research Director** Céline Wojtala
**Prepress Desktop Specialist** Paige King
**Color Quality Analyst** Pamela Powers

### MEREDITH SPECIAL INTEREST MEDIA
**Vice President & Group Publisher** Scott Mortimer
**Vice President, Group Editorial Director** Stephen Orr
**Vice President, Marketing** Jeremy Biloon
**Executive Account Director** Doug Stark
**Director, Brand Marketing** Jean Kennedy
**Sales Director** Christi Crowley
**Associate Director, Brand Marketing** Bryan Christian
**Senior Brand Manager** Katherine Barnet

**Editorial Director** Kostya Kennedy
**Creative Director** Gary Stewart
**Director of Photography** Christina Lieberman
**Editorial Operations Director** Jamie Roth Major
**Manager, Editorial Operations** Gina Scauzillo

**Special thanks** Brad Beatson, Melissa Frankenberry,
Samantha Lebofsky, Kate Roncinske, Laura Villano

### MEREDITH NATIONAL MEDIA GROUP
**President** Jon Werther
**President, Meredith Magazines** Doug Olson
**President, Consumer Products** Tom Witschi
**President, Chief Digital Officer** Catherine Levene
**Chief Revenue Officer** Michael Brownstein
**Chief Marketing & Data Officer** Alysia Borsa
**Marketing & Integrated Communications** Nancy Weber

### SENIOR VICE PRESIDENTS
**Consumer Revenue** Andy Wilson
**Corporate Sales** Brian Kightlinger
**Direct Media** Patti Follo
**Research Solutions** Britta Cleveland
**Strategic Sourcing, Newsstand, Production** Chuck Howell
**Digital Sales** Marla Newman
**Product & Technology** Justin Law

### VICE PRESIDENTS
**Finance** Chris Susil
**Business Planning & Analysis** Rob Silverstone
**Consumer Marketing** Steve Crowe
**Shopper Marketing** Carol Campbell
**Brand Licensing** Steve Grune

**Vice President, Group Editorial Director** Stephen Orr
**Director, Editorial Operations & Finance** Greg Kayko

### MEREDITH CORPORATION
**President & Chief Executive Officer** Tom Harty
**Chief Financial Officer** Joseph Ceryanec
**Chief Development Officer** John Zieser
**President, Meredith Local Media Group** Patrick McCreery
**Senior Vice President, Human Resources** Dina Nathanson

**Chairman** Stephen M. Lacy
**Vice Chairman** Mell Meredith Frazier

**PHOTO CREDITS**
**COVER:** Lee: Matt Sayles/AP/Shutterstock; Spider-Man: Entertainment Pictures/Zuma; Hulk: ©Marvel/©Walt Disney Studios Motion Pictures/Everett
Collection; Black Panther, Iron Man: ©Walt Disney Studios Motion Pictures/Everett Collection (2); **BACK COVER:** Santi Visalli/Getty Images; Inside Front Cover:
JHPhoto/Alamy; **1:** United News/Popperfoto/Getty Images; **2-3:** Kevin Winter/Getty Images; **4-5:** Charley Gallay/Getty Images; **6-7:** Moviestore Collection/
Shutterstock; **8-9:** AF Archive/Alamy; Silver Surfer: Fox/Marvel/Kobal/Shutterstock; **10-11:** J. Boland/Marvel Studios/Kobal/Shutterstock; **12:** Marvel/
Disney/Kobal/Shutterstock; **13:** Moviestore Collection/Shutterstock; **14-15:** Daredevil: Barry Wechter/Netflix; Doctor Strange: Album/Alamy; **16-17:** X-Men
Apocalypse: Pictorial Press Ltd./Alamy; Stewart: Entertainment Pictures/Alamy; Marsden and Janssen: Collection Christophel/Alamy; Hardy: TCD/Prod.DB/
Alamy; **18-19:** Marvel/Disney/Kobal/Shutterstock; **20-21:** Stan Lee Papers/American Heritage Center/University of Wyoming; **22:** United News/Popperfoto/
Getty Images; **24:** with Joan: REX/Shutterstock; with Joan Celia: Alberto E. Rodriguez/Getty Images; **25:** AP/Shutterstock; **26:** ©Marvel (2); **27:** Rick Meyer/Los
Angeles Times/Polaris; **28:** Nick Ut/AP/Shutterstock; **29:** Iron Man: Denise Truscello/Getty Images; throne: Lester Cohen/WireImage; Spidey: Ringo Chiu/Zuma;
**31-32:** Gerald Martineau/The Washington Post/Getty Images; **32-33:** Joseph Kubes/Alamy; **34:** Katy Winn/Invision/AP/REX/Shutterstock; **35:** Todd Wawrychuk/
Disney XD/Getty Images; **36:** Evan Hurd/Alamy; **38-39:** William E. Sauro/The New York Times/Redux; **40:** ©Marvel; **41:** Moviestore Collection/Shutterstock;
**42:** ©Marvel; **43:** Moviestore Collection/Shutterstock; **44:** ©Marvel; **45:** ©Walt Disney Studios Motion Pictures/Photofest; **48-49:** Kerry Hayes/20th Century
Fox/Kobal/Shutterstock; **50:** Buck/EPA/REX/Shutterstock; **52-53:** BEI/REX Shutterstock; **54:** Comic Con:Jason Merritt/FilmMagic; on set: 20th Century Fox/
Marvel/Kobal/REX/Shutterstock; **55:** ©20thCentFox/Everett Collection; **56:** Ant Man: Kevin Winter/Getty Images; Webb: ©Columbia Pictures/Photofest;
**57:** AF Archive/Alamy; **58-59:** Max Kennedy/ABC Family/Getty Images; **60:** Disney XD/Getty Images (2); **61:** Chris Haston/Universal; **62-63:** Family Guy:
©Fox Digital Entertainment/Photofest; Mallrats: ©Gramercy Pictures/Photofest; Big Bang Theory: Cliff Lipson/CBS/Getty Images; **64-65:** Simpsons: FOX/Getty
Images; FOTB: Richard Cartwright/ABC/Getty Images; Spider-Man 2: Columbia/Kobal/REX/Shutterstock; **66-67:** Charley Gallay/Getty Images; **68-69:** Courtesy
Todd McFarlane; **70-71:** Matt Winkelmeyer/Getty Images; **72-73:** clockwise: Chris Pizzello/Invision/AP/REX/Shutterstock; Albert L. Ortega/Getty Images; Victor
Chavez/WireImage; Dennis Poroy/AP; **74-75:** clockwise: Michael Buckner/Variety/REX/Shutterstock; Bei/REX/Shutterstock; Jonathan Leibson/FilmMagic; Rich
Polk/Getty Images; Gabriel Olsen/Getty Images; **76-77:** clockwise: Courtesy Charlotte Norris; Albert L. Ortega/Getty Images (2); Courtesy Nicholas Beecher;
Courtesy Saswata, Susruta and Satadru Mukherjee; Joaquin Sarmiento/AFP/Getty Images; **78-79:** Tom Levy/San Francisco Chronicle/Polaris; **80:** Eugene Garcia/
EPA-EFE/REX/Shutterstock; Inside Back Cover: Joseph Kubes/Alamy

▲
Stan Lee, then
publisher of
Marvel Comics, in
California in 1987.

# On Bended Knee

Stan Lee didn't create Captain America (that credit goes to writer-editor Joe Simon and writer-artist Jack Kirby), but he began contributing to the patriotic superhero's voice at age 18, in the 1941 "Captain America Foils the Traitor's Revenge." That tale featured the earliest time the Captain used his shield as a projectile, which went on to be a major plot point in 1964, when Lee teamed up with Kirby to resurrect the supersoldier. Here, Captain America, far from his New York City home, lays flowers on Lee's star on the Hollywood Walk of Fame.